02552

GROGAN'S
CASE STUDIES
in reference work

1 Enquiries and the reference process

GROGAN'S CASE STUDIES
in reference work

1 Enquiries and the reference process

Denis Grogan

Head of the Department of Bibliographical Studies
College of Librarianship Wales

CLIVE BINGLEY  LONDON

© Denis Joseph Grogan 1987

Published by
Clive Bingley Limited
7 Ridgmount Street
London WC1E 7AE

Case studies in reference work published 1967
More case studies in reference work published 1972
Grogan's case studies in reference work. Volume 1 first published 1987

British Library Cataloguing in Publication Data

Grogan, Denis
    Grogan's case studies in reference work.
    Vol. 1: Enquiries and the reference
    process
    1. Reference services (Libraries)
    I. Title
    025.5'2   Z711

    ISBN 0–85157–364–9

Phototypeset in 10/12 Linotron Times by
Input Typesetting Ltd, London SW19 8DR
Printed and made in Great Britain by
Redwood Burn Ltd, Trowbridge, Wiltshire

CONTENTS

v

FOREWORD

As my *Case studies in reference work* (1967) had been out-of-print for ten years and copies of *More case studies in reference work* (1972) were virtually exhausted, I welcomed my publisher's invitation to produce a new sequence which would be an updated blend of the text used in the two earlier volumes to introduce and comment on the cases but would provide completely new cases to illustrate the points made. The result is a short series on the following plan:

1. Enquiries and the reference process
2. Encyclopedias, yearbooks, directories, and statistical sources
3. Bibliographies of books
4. Periodicals and their guides
5. Dictionaries and phrase books
6. Biographical sources

So far as concerns the *text*, therefore, the series can be regarded as a revised and amalgamated version of the two earlier works, but so far as concerns the new *cases*, it is best seen as a continuation, since many of the 345 cases in the earlier volumes remain relevant for their purpose, and by students with access to them can still be read with advantage as illustrations of the way in which reference sources are used to help enquirers.

The assumption underlying the approach I have adopted is that reference work cannot be taught, at least not solely by means of instruction. This is because it is an art, and skill within an art depends on practice, not precept. Of course, like many other professional arts, such as advocacy or medicine, it rests on a basis of science, that is to say a body of theoretic truth, of connected facts. For the reference librarian or information worker this body of principles is the science of systematic bibliography, and it is this that makes up the foundation of their professional education.

Like all intellectual disciplines, it is acquired by study. But the art of reference work, defined as personal assistance to individual users in pursuit of information, or even more simply, finding information somebody has asked for, can only be learned by experience.

There is no substitute for experience: the only way to obtain it in any field is to engage in activity in that field. This is particularly true for the librarian: Margaret Hutchins writes plainly: 'In no occupation does one learn more on the job than in reference work.' Nevertheless, just as the would-be lawyer or the medical student may gain at least some insight into the art of advocacy or of medicine by the observation of cases, either actual (in the courts or at the bedside) or reported (in the books), so it is possible for the student librarian to begin to appreciate the art of reference work by looking over the shoulder of an experienced practitioner, either actually working on a problem in the library, or as written up afterwards in a book of case histories.

With this object in mind these case notes in the use of information sources have been compiled. It is hoped that they will serve to illuminate the more theoretical study of bibliographical control and of the sources of recorded information which provide the scientific basis for reference work. It should be said that all these cases represent genuine enquiries, in the sense that they contain questions that have all been asked (and answered) in real library situations. Of course, like all case notes, they were written up after the event, and no doubt hindsight has played some part in the way they are presented here. To enhance their value for teaching purposes, some have been deliberately brought up to date. Comment too has occasionally been added, where it seemed it might shed light: for example, alternative paths to the answer have sometimes been explored for the sake of comparison, and often a note has been appended about new information traced or published after the enquiry was completed.

The information sources demonstrated in the series have as a rule been limited to general reference works such as encyclopedias, yearbooks, and directories, dictionaries and phrase books, and biographical dictionaries; and to general (mostly national) bibliographies and multidisciplinary periodical indexes. However, the student will notice that in a number of the cases the information sources consulted include machine-readable databases searched online, a facility unavailable when the 1967 and 1972 texts were being written. Enthusiasts would probably like to have seen more of these enquiries resolved by a computer search, and several could have been; as I myself wrote in *Practical reference work* (1979), 'on-line searching has added a major weapon to the reference librarian's arsenal'.

But despite its high profile in the professional literature, actual searching (as opposed to the availability of search facilities) has advanced only slowly in libraries. Even in quite large and busy institutions, answering perhaps half-a-million or more enquiries annually, online searches carried out each year are to be counted in hundreds rather than thousands. A survey of 500 university and college libraries in the United States chosen at random reported in 1986 that well over half provided no online searching at all and of the minority that did offer the service 44 per cent carried out less than 100 searches a year. Only 5.8 per cent did more than 1,000 searches in a year. In 1986 applicants for posts in the Reference Libraries of the BBC, by no means technological sluggards, were advised that 'Most enquiries are still answered from traditional printed sources.'

Reasons for the slow advance of online searching in libraries are several, among them being cost and a lingering degree of staff reluctance. But foremost is the fact that the vast majority of reference enquiries are simply not susceptible to an online search, even if funds were unlimited and staff had the best will in the world. It is no coincidence that the highest proportion of online use – commonly around 15 per cent of the total searches – is to be found in medical libraries and in information services in science-based industry, where a wide range of relevant databases has been available for well over a decade. But this is changing: the number of databases, and even more importantly, the spread of subjects and genres covered, continue to increase rapidly, reflected at a more deliberate pace by the numbers of online searches carried out in libraries. A particular boost in recent years has been provided by the recognition that over and above formalized by-appointment online searching on a fee-paying basis there is a distinct role for the computer in impromptu everyday reference searching, in verifying garbled or incomplete citations, for instance, or tracing current information too recent for printed sources, or quickly locating two or three relevant items on an obscure topic or by a specific author, and so on. Even so, such searches still represent only a miniscule proportion of all reference searches. A 1984 survey of such database use at the reference desks of 160 United States libraries of all types found that online ready-reference questions were only 2.4 per cent of the number of general reference questions.

Online searching therefore has not yet transformed reference work, as some predicted it would; still less has it eliminated the reference librarian altogether. Nevertheless, it has become plain that the ability to interrogate a computerized database is now a requirement for the compleat reference librarian as more and more additional reference tools – encylopedias, directories, biographical dictionaries, as well as bibliographies and indexes – are becoming available in machine-readable format. And access may not be limited to distant databases that have to be searched over telecommunications links. Already the advent of compact disc read-only-memory technology interfaced with a microcomputer is allowing the reference librarian to sever this particular umbilical cord. We are told that one 4.75 inch diameter disc can comfortably accommodate the whole of *Encyclopaedia Britannica* in digital form, and the MARC databases are already being marketed in this CD-ROM format. A CD-ROM version of the *Oxford English dictionary* is already in preparation. Such distributed databases, being completely self-contained, can be used as often as needed, without extra cost, like printed sources. And as microfiche is already doing, they may even come to replace the printed versions of certain bibliographical and reference sources.

This series however, as a record of actual cases, perforce has to describe what is found, not what might be. It is interesting to note that in none of the cases recounted in another compilation from the same publisher, M. J. Campbell, *Case studies in business information provision* (1983), was an online search necessary. As the author explains, this was simply because 'For whatever reason, none of the contributors, most of whom have access to a terminal of some kind, submitted any cases resolved by this means.' But the online enthusiast can take comfort from the fact that there are thousands of sample searches (though not case studies) to be found in the online textbooks and in the manuals produced by the database producers and online service suppliers.

The application of 'the case method' in teaching librarianship has been considerably extended since the experiments in 1951 at the School of Library Science, Simmons College, Boston, under Professor Kenneth R. Shaffer, and there are now scores of published collections of cases in many fields of librarianship. It is worth emphasizing, however, that there are several kinds of cases and several methods of using them. One interesting variety, deriving from the method pioneered at the Harvard Business School, is the case presented as a 'situation' or 'problem' for which the student is encouraged to suggest a solution (or indeed solutions, for there are often several). The case histories in this series and my previous collections derive from a much older tradition, best exemplified in the legal and medical textbooks, and pioneered in librarianship by Herbert Woodbine, whose contributions to the 'Reference libraries' column of the *Library Association record* from May 1936 to December 1944 are filled with accounts of how actual reference questions were answered. The first textbook to contain case studies was S. R. Ranganathan, *Reference service*, published at Madras in 1940. These are *resolved* cases, complete descriptions of particular problems from start to finish, including the solutions arrived at.

But the use of case studies to teach reference work has not been without its misunderstandings. It is not sufficiently realized that the compiler of a collection of cases cannot proceed merely by objective sampling, however scientifically performed. Each case must be subjectively chosen to demonstrate a specific point, and, ideally, to illustrate a particular principle of general application. For instance, it is an observable fact that often when asked for information on a particular subject (such as fire brigades, or haiku, or silhouettes) the reference librarian will immediately recall to mind a specific book devoted to the topic. Furthermore, he (or more usually she) may be able to locate it right away on the shelves, without benefit of catalogue or bibliography or reference book. I have myself done just this hundreds of times. But there is no profit in describing such an incident in a case study. For one thing, despite the glow that one feels at the time, it is no more reference work than the post office clerk producing on request a stamp of the right denomination or the assistant in the shoe store finding a pair to fit your particular feet. To maintain otherwise is to reduce this area of the reference librarian's art to a mere memory skill. But even more importantly, the narration of such an event as a case history *does not teach the student anything about reference method*, for, however frequently it occurs in practice, it does not illustrate any principle that can be applied in a wider context.

These cases therefore by no means represent a cross-section of questions asked. On the contrary, they have been hand-picked to illustrate in as precise a manner as possible the way the librarian uses general reference sources and bibliographies to help solve readers' problems. A truly representative sample would contain, in the first place, a large minority of questions answered from non-reference sources such as textbooks and monographs (for to equate reference work with the mere manipulation of reference books is to understate the case at least by half). In the second place, there would be many questions in such a selection that could not be answered from these *general* sources at all, but only from special or subject sources, such as dictionaries of engineering, or bibliographies of music, or business databases. This limitation to general sources of information, mainly in the English language, was thought appropriate for an introductory text, but it has meant, for instance, little mention of maps, atlases and gazetteers, since these are subject sources; hardly any reference to abstracting services, since these are all in specific subject fields; and where periodical indexes are discussed these are limited to titles such as *British humanities index* or *Applied science and technology index* rather than, say, *Index to legal periodicals* or *Chemical titles*. An adequate illustration of the way special and subject sources are used would demand another book, or indeed a series of books. It goes without saying that this limitation to the general sector applies only to the sources used and not to the questions treated in the cases. These range from Alexander Anderson to Zeppelin and Zwingli and from 2800 BC to events a year hence.

Neither are these cases set up as models to be copied. This is not a 'how-to-do-it' series: its aim is descriptive not prescriptive. These are actual problems and actual searches, chosen simply to illuminate the reference process by showing how reference sources *have been used* in real situations. Sometimes the librarian performs well, and sometimes not so well. He, or she, may even on occasion go astray; although I have of course tried to exclude instances where gross errors were committed or unreliable answers given.

In most cases the method set forth is only one of several alternative ways of reaching the same solution. In many cases, no doubt, there are better methods. In those few cases, even, where the search was unsuccessful, another searcher tackling the problem afresh may quite well find the way to the answer. These examples, then, are illustrations to be studied, and not necessarily patterns to be followed.

Many of the enquiries will be familiar to experienced reference librarians: one of the phenomena noticed by students of the reference process is the intriguing way in which highly abstruse or seemingly unique questions are repeated at various times and in various places in libraries of all kinds.

Many of these cases will also be familiar to my own students: I would like to thank those who have taken the postgraduate and undergraduate courses at the College of Librarianship Wales for their interest and forbearance over several years.

Aberystwyth   **D. J. Grogan**
June 1986

INTRODUCTION

The 51 cases in this first volume in the series *Grogan's case studies in reference work* have been selected to illustrate the various categories of enquiry that are received by reference librarians and to demonstrate the methods they use to satisfy them. An adequate response will often involve detailed discussion with the enquirer, close analysis of the topic, a carefully constructed search strategy, and a painstaking search. The assistance of colleagues is sometimes needed and a flexible approach is essential always.

Although the topics treated in these cases range over the whole field of knowledge, the emphasis in this first volume is on the form and nature of the enquiry rather than the subject-matter or the sources used to supply the answer. Later volumes in this series will focus on sources, illustrating in turn the ways in which the general bibliographies and periodical indexes and the major categories of reference works such as encyclopedias, dictionaries, yearbooks, biographical dictionaries, and the like, are drawn upon by librarians to help solve their enquirers' problems.

ENQUIRIES

The skill that reference librarians show in analysing the queries that they receive is a key factor in their success in providing satisfactory responses. In the next section something will be said about analysing the subject of an enquiry, but first an account should be given of the methods of grading questions according to the complexity of the information required. What follows is one of many such groupings, that has been found useful for purposes of study.

Author/title enquiries

The enquirer here is seeking a *particular work* and little needs to be said about these since most libraries are designed to answer such questions immediately from the catalogue, e.g., 'Have you a copy of *The perfect lady* by Feng Meng Lung?' or 'Do you take the *AORN journal?*'

Factual enquiries

These are perhaps more descriptively called 'fact-finding' enquiries, e.g., 'What is the average weight of the human male brain?' (1,409 grams or 49.7 ounces, from *New encyclopaedia Britannica*); 'When were the first Nobel Prizes awarded?' (10th December 1901, from *Information please almanac*); 'What is a Bath Oliver?' (an unsweetened biscuit invented by Dr W. Oliver of Bath, died 1764, from *Concise Oxford dictionary*); 'Do they have Justices of the Peace in Canada?' (yes, in *Statesman's yearbook*).

The answer is usually a specific item of information, but this does not mean that such queries are easy to solve. Although they are sometimes referred to as 'quick-reference' or 'ready-reference' questions, they may require a lengthy search, as these first two cases illustrate:

1

Case 1: 'What was the last country to join the United Nations?' was the clear and unambiguous question posed in a Merseyside reference library. Obviously one definitive reference work on the subject would be the *Year book of the United Nations*, but when the librarian went to consult it she discovered – or thought she had discovered – that the library's copy was some years out of date. However, closer examination revealed that the work itself was running late, with a date of publication some three years after the nominal year covered. The current *Statesman's year-book* as anticipated provided an alphabetical list of all 157 UN members, but gave neither dates of joining nor an indication of how up-to-date the list was. The information provided by *Whitaker's almanack* was exactly similar.

In the *Europa yearbook*, however, the list of names (also 157) included 'year of admission'. A rapid scanning of the list located the three newest members, all admitted in 1981: Antigua and Barbuda, Belize, and Vanuatu. The librarian was interested to note in passing the list of 'Sovereign countries not in the United Nations': these were 12 in number, ranging from Andorra to Vatican City, of which the most surprising (to her) was Switzerland. Helpfully, the date of the information was given as October 1982. It therefore remained to check two points: had any other nations been admitted since? and if not, which of the three 1981 candidates was the most recent?

Such matters would obviously have been reported in the newspapers, to which the librarian turned next, starting in fact with a news *digest* service, *Keesing's contemporary archives*. A careful check of the indexes under 'United Nations' from 1981 up to the current monthly issue for March 1984 located nothing more recent than the admission of Antigua and Barbuda as the 157th member after it had gained its independence from Britain on 1st November 1981. Remembering however that *Keesing's* is only a digest service, with an index of doubtful reliability, the librarian also checked the *Times index*, in this case working backwards from March 1984. Within a few moments she found in the September 1983 issue an entry under 'United Nations org.' referring to the admission of St Kitts-Nevis. The item in *The Times* proved to be no more than six lines in the issue for 23rd September about the unanimous approval given by the UN to the admission of 'Saint

Christopher and Nevis' a few days after it had achieved independence. Curious as to why this had been missed by *Keesing's* the
librarian checked the index once more, but this time under 'St
Kitts-Nevis'. There she found in the issue for December 1983 a
reference to 'attainment of full independence'. Following this up
she found two full pages of text, complete with map, including
the information that 'on Sept. 23 it became the 158th member of
the United Nations'. With this her enquirer expressed himself
totally satisfied, though she felt obliged to point out that there
may well have been other admissions in the four or five weeks
since the latest monthly issue of the *Times index*; she went on to
add that the daily issues of *The Times* were available for scanning
if he wished to take the trouble.

Case 2:   The enquirer in a large city public library seeking the
founder-members of the Independent Labour Party said he had
had no luck with *Encyclopaedia Britannica*. Asked by the reference librarian if he had tried any of the British encyclopaedias,
the enquirer was amazed to learn that *Britannica* had been an
American publication for most of the present century. As he
had in fact consulted only *Britannica* the librarian took him to
Chambers's encyclopaedia, where they found six references in the
index. In the main article they read that the party had been
'formed under the leadership of Keir Hardie at Bradford, Yorkshire, in 1893'. No other founders were mentioned, but the article
was followed by four bibliographical references of which the most
promising was H. Pelling, *The origins of the Labour Party,
1880–1900* (1954).

A copy of Pelling's book was then examined. The index had
some 30 references to the Independent Labour Party, including
one directing them to the 11 pages describing its foundation. This
was a full account of the inaugural conference at the Bradford
Labour Institute on 13th January 1893 attended by some 120
delegates, overwhelmingly from the industrial north of England
and from Scotland. A dozen or so names were mentioned in the
narrative, and in the caption to the photograph of the members
elected by the meeting to form the Council, all the 15 members
and the Secretary were named. Curiously, Keir Hardie was not
among them. Nowhere in the book could a list be discovered of

the 'founders', which the librarian and his enquirer had by now agreed meant all the delegates at the conference. The work carried no bibliography, apart from a 'List of unpublished sources consulted', but there were many footnotes, including one referring to the official *Report*. This was identified in the British Library *General catalogue of printed books* as *Report (minutes) General (annual) conference* (1893–1936).

After a further consultation with his enquirer, who seemed genuinely anxious to pursue the matter, the librarian called the local university library to see if they had a copy of the *Report* that they might be willing to lend, for consultation in the reference library only if they preferred. Their reply was that they did not; but then they added helpfully that they had a microfilm copy of the British Library set of *Annual reports* from 1893 that the enquirer was welcome to come and see. When this was in due course consulted, the first item was indeed found to be the *Report of the first general conference* (price one penny) held at Bradford on 13th and 14th January 1893. The first page of the text stated: '115 Delegates were present at the opening, the composition of the Conference being as follows' – and then followed the full list of names.

The majority of enquiries in libraries of all types are for this kind of 'pin-point' information. Of the remainder, a large proportion fall into the next category.

Subject enquiries
These are perhaps more accurately described as 'material-finding' queries, e.g., 'Can you find me something on Islamic attitudes to women?' or 'Have you anything on the use of music in treating mental illness?' or 'Can you suggest some books on the origins of the feudal system?' or 'What have you got on Capodimonte porcelain?'

From the librarian's point of view these 'something-on-a-subject' enquiries have two features: the result of the search is a bibliography, i.e., a list of references to sources of information (more often than not accompanied by the production of the material as required by the reader); secondly, since there can be

4

no definitive 'answer', the point is never reached where more material might not be discovered by further search.

It will be found that many enquiries of this kind come from readers who are quite well-versed in the literature of their own subject but need the librarian's help when starting 'reconnaissance' reading in a new field. These are particularly common in university and college libraries.

Case 3:   The reference librarian in a west of England county library found that the catalogue had nothing to offer the enquirer seeking information on fair organs, and neither, at first sight, had the encyclopedias – *New Britannica, Chambers's, Everyman's, World book, Academic American/Macmillan family*. Of course she had found many references to fairs and to organs, but none linking the two; then she remembered that in the first encyclopedia she had tried, the *Micropaedia* volumes of *New Britannica*, under 'organ' there had been references to 'related entries' on a dozen or so organ types. On consulting this list again she found that one name stirred a memory – 'calliope'. Was this not what the Americans called a fair organ? She pursued the reference. Calliope was not only one of the nine muses, patron of epic poetry, and the name of a rocket launcher of the 1940s, it was also a 'steam-whistle organ with a loud, shrill sound audible miles away; used to attract attention for circuses and fairs'. It had been invented in the United States about 1850 by A. S. Denny and patented in 1855 by Joshua C. Stoddard. A black-and-white photograph of 1908 showed a horse-drawn example in a parade.

Rechecking the other encyclopedias she found that the only Calliope known to *Chambers's* and *Everyman's* was the muse, but *World book* had a black-and-white line illustration of a steam organ and four lines of description, and *Academic American/ Macmillan family* had an eight-line article under 'calliope', claiming that its sound can be heard at a distance of up to 19 km (12 miles). More significantly, the bibliography cited A. W. J. G. Ord-Hume, *Clockwork music* (1973). Checking the library catalogue as a matter of routine the librarian was pleasantly surprised to locate a copy, and quite astonished when she came to examine it to discover that it was a British work by a founder-member of the Musical Box Society of Great Britain and the editor of its journal *The music box*. A fascinating compilation, illustrated throughout with facsimile reproductions of advertisements, pamphlets, journal articles and announcements, it had disappointingly little on calliopes, which was puzzling in the light of its citation in the bibliography in *Academic American/ Macmillan family encyclopedia*. Its index had no reference to fair organs, and only two page references to calliopes. The first was an illustrated trade announcement from the 4th December 1926 issue of *The billboard* showing 'The Han-Dee true tone calliope for rides, rinks, shows, fairs, boats, bands, and outside advertising'. The author's seven-line caption briefly outlined its history and invention by Stoddard. The second reference was to the facsimile of a page from the *Illustrated London news* of 3rd December 1859, showing a large illustration of 'The Calliope, or steam organ' on the occasion of its exhibition for the first time in England at the Crystal Palace, London. The 43 lines of accompanying text included the information that 'the Pasha of Egypt has one fixed on board his private steamer'.

The work had no bibliography but the publisher's blurb mentioned the author's forthcoming *Barrel organ*. This time there was no copy in the library catalogue, but a check through the *British national bibliography* forward from 1973 soon located it in the 1979 volume, subtitled *the story of the mechanical organ and its repair*, a substantial volume of 567 pages. When in due course a copy was obtained for the enquirer it proved to be all that he could have wished for, illustrated with 115 plates and 144 figures in the text. It made the interesting claim that 'Despite the host of books written on the king of instruments [i.e., the organ], none has ever been published dealing with the fascinating field of the mechanical organ.' Even more interestingly the author acknowledged the help of 'the last fair-organ builder in London'. A 33-page chapter was devoted to the fair organ, opening with the words, 'The subject of this chapter is a facet of the mechanical organ which is not generally recognised by the majority of writers on organs.' And as this work did have a bibliography the librarian was able to point out to her enquirer the two earlier books listed there, should be wish to pursue his quest further: *The fair organ and how it works* (1967) and *The fairground organ* (1970), both by E. V. Cockayne.

[An alternative approach might have been to search the *British national bibliography* subject index back to 1950. Checking under 'fair(s)' and 'organ(s)' would have located both works by Cockayne, but not *Clockwork music* (though it does have a main entry). The search would also have brought to light A. Beaumont, *Fair organs: 50 pictures* (1968), *The key frame: the journal of the Fair Organ Preservation Society* (1964–), *Steam and organ year-book* (1976–), and one or two other minor works.]

Case 4: 'Have you anything on the runic alphabet?' was the way the young enquirer put her question in a Midlands reference library. While leading her towards the encyclopedias the librarian sensibly enquired further, learning that she was a student of Old English who had been set a piece of work on the subject. The appropriate *Micropaedia* volume of *New encyclopaedia Britannica* had a full column on this 'writing system of uncertain origin used by Germanic peoples of northern Europe, Britain, Scandinavia and Iceland from about the 3rd century to the 16th or 17th century AD'. It seemed to the librarian a fairly complex subject, with at least three main varieties, common Germanic, Anglo-Saxon and Nordic, and over 4,000 runic inscriptions and several runic manu-scripts extant, but his enquirer narrowed it down for him by saying she was only interested in the Anglo-Saxon version. The *Micropaedia* entry referred the reader to the main article on 'alphabets' in the *Macropaedia*, where half a column was found on the topic with a comparative table showing the runic alphabet alongside the Latin, Greek, Cyrillic, etc., alphabets. All this the student found interesting of course, but she obviously needed much more; the *Macropaedia* bibliography listed a couple of dozen works on alphabets, but nothing specific on runic.

The subject index to the library catalogue showed nothing on the runic alphabet, so the librarian decided that a search of the *British national bibliography* was called for, starting with the latest issues, and working backwards. Subject entries for 'runes' and 'runic writing' were found immediately, but these concerned 'occult aspects' or led to titles like *The runes and other magic alphabets*, and works like the 13-page unpriced pamphlet published by Megalithic Visions. This was clearly not the kind of material the enquirer wanted, but the search was continued. Within a few moments the librarian was able to suggest two likely titles: R. W. V. Elliott, *Runes: an introduction*, a 1980 reprint of a 1963 publication from Manchester University Press, and R. I. Page, *An introduction to English runes* (1973), a 253-page work from the long-established publishing house of Methuen. The grateful enquirer made a careful note of the details and said she would try to get them from the college library.

[Had the librarian moved on to the British encyclopedias after consulting *New Britannica* he would have found in *Everyman's* an excellent and scholarly short article with a 14-item bibliography, including both Elliott and Page.

Elliott's work has 140 pages and 24 full-page photographic plates. Chapter IV 'Runic writing in England' is 13 pages long and Chapter VII 'Some English runic inscriptions' has 34 pages. Both have extensive bibliographies. Page's book, devoted entirely to English runes, has a detailed bibliography and is written for 'the informed beginner'.]

Research enquiries

It has been said that 'to look in one book is reference, in two books is search, in three books is research', but true research involves more than mere hunting. The essence of successful research is that something is added to the store of human knowledge: either a completely new discovery, such as a method of using sunlight to split water into oxygen and hydrogen as a source of cheap fuel; or on the other hand, the rediscovery of something that has been lost, such as the Roman road from Chester into Wales, or the score of *Thespis*, Gilbert and Sullivan's first collaboration.

In most libraries true research is beyond the call of duty for the librarian. If it is discovered that the reader's problem cannot be solved either from the literature or from the various other sources of information, documentary and oral, and the librarian has indeed reached the frontiers of knowledge, then their ways must usually part. The level of the librarian's participation stays at material-finding, though this may of course extend to primary sources such as unpublished letters and diaries. But it is for the research worker alone to evaluate such material, to investigate the evidence, to form the conclusions. That is not to say that librarians never work at this exalted level. In certain libraries they frequently do: but they are not practising the art of reference work, they are doing research.

Case 5: The librarian's first reaction to a question in a large public reference library about spontaneous human combustion was incredulity. She was by no means convinced when her enquirer assured her that he did indeed mean 'people bursting into flame', but she agreed to make a search. Though she found 'spontaneous combustion' treated in most of the encyclopedias she checked (*New Britannica, Collier's, Everyman's, World book, Academic American/Macmillan family*), the descriptions referred to the phenomenon in hay, coal and other obviously combustible materials, but not in humans. It was not until she turned to the great *Oxford English dictionary* that she encountered the first piece of evidence that she was not wasting her time: she learned that 'spontaneous combustion' was also used in the special sense of 'the alleged occurrence of this fact in persons addicted to the excessive use of alcohol'. Five quotations to illustrate this meaning were given, ranging from 1795 to 1822, the last of which (from H. Power and L. W. Sedgwick, *Lexicon of medicine and allied subjects*) added the dismissive comment: 'In most of the cases recorded . . . either they have been near a fire, or some suspicious circumstances suggestive of murder have been present.'

As the library catalogue had nothing to offer, the librarian was at something of a loss where to turn next. Wisely, she consulted a senior colleague, evoking her instant response: 'There was a letter in *The Times* about that a year or so ago.' This was too good a lead to ignore, though it did take longer than anticipated to follow it up. As so often, it was less recent than the colleague had remembered, but eventually in the *Index* under 'fires: spontaneous combustion' a letter was located in *The Times* issue for 23rd October 1982 from the Professor of Combustion Physics, Imperial College, London, obviously a sceptic, asking for details of the phenomenon which had been referred to in an earlier account by Peter Ackroyd on 16th October. The librarian could not at first trace this earlier reference – it was not under 'fires' or under 'Ackroyd' in the *Index* – and it required a page-by-page scan to find it. It was discovered embedded in Ackroyd's regular

9

television column – unindexed because *The Times* as a matter of policy does not index staff contributors by name. Reviewing a programme on UFOs (unidentified flying objects), he commented on a similar unexplained phenomenon: 'It is also possible that certain human beings can project energy outwards from themselves, and that it can take a solid or recognizable form – certainly the cases of spontaneous combustion, when an individual bursts into flame, suggest that such energy exists and can consume its carrier.' The *Index* revealed only one response to the professor's request for evidence, not from Ackroyd himself but in another letter a few days later. This correspondent reminded readers of the similar doubts that had been raised following the publication of *Bleak House* by Charles Dickens where the death of Mr Krook from this cause was described: 'Dickens assured the sceptics that he had taken pains to investigate the subject thoroughly and had discovered 30 recorded cases', at (among other places), Verona, Rheims and Columbus, Ohio.

Recalling that one of the *OED* quotations had in fact been from *Bleak House* (1853), the librarian thought that this might be a fruitful line to pursue. The *New Cambridge bibliography of English literature*, volume 3 (1969), does of course treat *Bleak House*, and among the references cited under 'Studies' the librarian discovered G. S. Haight, 'Dickens and Lewes on spontaneous combustion' in *Nineteenth-century fiction*, **10** (1956). This 11-page article was found to give an account of the controversial series of exchanges in print between Dickens and George Henry Lewes who 'made it his business to attack any superstition that raised its head'. Haight's conclusion was that 'This discussion of spontaneous combustion gives a striking example of the intellectual limitations that made [Dickens] indifferent or hostile to the scientific developments of his age.'

This was plainly a topic which would bear further investigation, with the *OED* fairly clearly in the camp of the unbelievers and *The Times* a hundred years later suggesting there might be some truth in the matter. The enquirer was now quite evidently more interested than ever in the subject, and though the librarian suspected that she would still be unable to resolve the issue she agreed to continue the search.

As an experienced reference librarian she knew that one obvious source to consult with this kind of enquiry was the famous periodical *Notes and queries*, subtitled *for readers and writers, collectors and librarians*, which according to E. P. Sheehy, *Guide to reference books*, 'contains a large amount of interesting and often very valuable information on out-of-the-way questions'. It took her no more than a few minutes to check the invaluable cumulated indexes back to 1849, where she retrieved over a dozen references. The earliest, in the issue for 19th March 1853 [i.e., while *Bleak House* was actually appearing in its 19 monthly parts], was a query from a correspondent who simply asked 'Is there such a thing as spontaneous combustion?' In the weeks that followed he received a variety of replies, ranging from a reference to the official medical report of a case in the *Journal of medical science*, December 1852, to a quotation from Taylor's *Medical jurisprudence* (1846): 'There is not a single well-authenticated instance of such an event occurring.' The latest index reference was to a response from the editor, quoting *Bleak House*, to a query in *American notes and queries* for September 1942 asking, 'Where are other accounts of this strange manner of death?' This evoked by way of a later response a quotation from Woodman and Tydy, *Forensic medicine*: 'There is no subject in the whole range of medical jurisprudence on which so much romance has been built.'

In the hope of possibly more recent periodical articles on this obviously disputed topic the librarian and her enquirer next mounted a two-pronged attack on the periodical indexes. She herself took *British humanities index*, starting with the most recent quarterly issue. Almost immediately under 'spontaneous combustion' she found an article entitled 'A burnt out case', in the *Spectator* for 18th/25th December 1982. Though there was nothing on the face of it to indicate that this was about *human* spontaneous combustion, the fact that the author's name was Peter Ackroyd suggested that it was likely. Consultation of the article itself soon confirmed that this was so, and also showed that since his comments in *The Times* two months previously Ackroyd had been in touch privately with the sceptical professor who had convinced him that 'It is of course scientifically impossible.' However, he pointed out that 'testimonies of its existence are still being received' and he prefaced his article with a quotation from the *Daily Telegraph* of 6th August 1982: 'A woman walking down a street in Chicago burst into flames for no apparent reason and was burned to death yesterday.' He went on to refer to other

11

cases, such as a 1938 incident at Chelmsford, mentioned *Bleak House*, and cited the 'first treatise on the subject, *De Incendiis Corporis Humanis Spontaneis* . . . published in 1763'. His conclusion was that in the absence of a sufficient explanation the question must remain open: 'The concept of human personality and of human life which spontaneous combustion implicitly asserts is darker and more mysterious than the scientific vision of the world.'

By now the librarian realized she was entering the area of the unknown, or at least of the still unanswered, and felt she must call a halt. Meanwhile, however, the enquirer, who had been set the task of working backwards from the current issue of *Readers' guide to periodical literature* looking under 'combustion, spontaneous', had himself found a reference to a 1981 article in *Science digest*: L. E. Arnold, 'Human fireballs [spontaneous human combustion]'. This he very much wanted to see and a copy was in due course obtained from another library. Of course, *Science digest* is a popular though respected US journal, and the three-page article was obviously written for the lay reader. Headed by the caption, 'For centuries, experts have attempted to solve the mystery of spontaneous human combustion', it referred to over 200 cases spanning four centuries, quoting chapter and verse (and including a photograph) for a 1966 case involving an invalid Pennsylvania physician, as well as similar instances in Pennsylvania in 1957 and Florida in 1951. The author by no means treated 'SHC', as he called it, as a question that had been resolved. His concluding paragraph read: 'Science works best when observations can be carefully controlled. Because of the nature of SHC, it has eluded such close scrutiny so far. Researchers have had to make do with anecdotal reports. . . . That some strange fiery fate has befallen selected individuals throughout history seems undeniable, but whether a rational explanation will fit with current scientific concepts or will open new doors to the unknown, only time and more study will tell.' The article also stated that its author was 'now at work' on *Ablaze! the incredible mystery of spontaneous human combustion*. To see whether this work had been published the librarian checked the microfiche *Books in English* from 1981 to April 1984, and then for good measure the microfiche *Books in print* of June 1984, but without success.

Mutable enquiries

In practice the librarian often finds that these categories shade one into the other. The straightforward author/title query may become a factual enquiry if the book or periodical requested is not found in the library catalogue. In such cases, instead of giving an immediate 'no' to the reader, it is a sound principle to look up particulars of the work. The substantive form of the question then is 'Are these bibliographical details correct, and if so, where can I see a copy?' In a surprisingly high proportion of cases it will be found that the library does have a copy after all.

Case 6: Asked in a central London public library for a copy of *The Lambton worm* the young librarian predictably asked the enquirer if she knew who the author was. She seemed a trifle puzzled by his question but admitted that she did not. The librarian therefore consulted the microfiche *British books in print*, which he knew did list books under title, and found a 64-page work of that title by T. Deary, published in 1981. No copy appeared in the library catalogue so he consulted the 1981 *British national bibliography* volumes in search of more information. The work was indeed listed, but the appended classification number, 823.914(J), indicated that it was children's fiction – and therefore not available in that particular library.

His explanation to the enquirer provoked the immediate response, 'Yes, I know that. It's a fairy story.' Apologizing at once, he swiftly recovered himself: this was a different matter altogether. He soon found half-a-dozen references to 'The Lambton worm' in M. H. Eastman, *Index to fairy tales, myths and legends* (2nd edition, 1926) and its various *Supplements* to 1977. Unfortunately, the library had copies of neither of the two most likely sources, E. S. Hartland, *English folk and fairy tales* and E. Rhys, *Fairy gold*. A few moments at the appropriate shelves, however, located the scholarly K. M. Briggs, *The personnel of fairyland* (1953), where he found the five-page story, illustrated with two delightful scraper-board drawings, of this queer fish-like monster caught by the Heir of Lambton in the River Wear, which eventually escaped to lay waste the countryside. A footnote cited W. Henderson, *Folk-lore of the northern counties of England and the borders.*

Similarly the hunt for a specific item of information sometimes widens into a search for material when the librarian discovers there is no cut-and-dried answer.

Case 7: 'I've got to find out the difference between herbs and spices. Can you help me, please?' was the plea late one evening from a young enquirer. *World book encyclopedia* seemed a good place to start and the librarian was gratified to find a separate article on 'herb' and another on 'spice'. Unfortunately, even a close reading of both accounts left librarian and enquirer still unsure as to the precise difference: the first simply said that 'Some herbs are used in cooking to flavour foods'; the second that spice is the 'name given to food seasonings made from plants'. The *Concise Oxford dictionary* was only a little more helpful: 'herb' was defined as 'plant of which leaves, etc. are used for food, scent, medicine, flavour, etc.' and 'spice' as 'aromatic or pungent vegetable substance used to flavour food'.

New encyclopaedia Britannica treated both together in one entry in the *Micropaedia*: 'Spices and herbs are flavourful parts of plants used in cooking.' It did, however, go on to draw one distinction: 'Spices such as cinnamon, cloves, and ginger originated in tropical or subtropical regions; herbs such as rosemary, marjoram, and thyme are native to the temperate zones.' But then the main text article in the *Macropaedia* warned, 'They are commonly spoken of loosely as spices, spice seeds, and herbs.' The only slight extra distinction made was that herbs are usually leaves, whereas spices can also be from other parts of the plants. Finally, in *Academic American/Macmillan family encyclopedia* the librarian found an excellent one-and-a-half column article, 'herbs and spices', illustrated and furnished with a nine-item bibliography. This neatly summed up the question as follows: 'Although the distinctions are not always clear-cut, spices are, in general, the products of tropical and subtropical trees, shrubs, or vines and are characterized by highly pungent odours or flavours. The fragrant leaves of

14

certain herbaceous plants of the temperate regions are called herbs.'

The material-finding enquiry too will occasionally spill over into research, as, for example, when a search for information on an obscure 19th-century artist exhausts the historical and biographical books, and the hunt switches to primary sources such as contemporary local newspapers and directories, and even census returns, parish registers and wills. Problems of this nature can indeed become so fascinating that librarians have often to restrain their sleuthing instincts in the interests of other calls on their time.

Case 8: An enquiry about the present whereabouts of the original ark sent the librarian in a north of England reference library straight to the encyclopedias. Immediately in *New Britannica (Micropaedia)* under 'ark of the Covenant' he was able to read about this 'ornate, gold-plated wooden chest that in biblical times housed the two tablets of the Law given to Moses by God'. Though it was taken to Jerusalem by King David and eventually placed in the Temple by King Solomon, 'The final fate of the ark is unknown.' To the librarian this seemed quite conclusive, and he was about to leave his enquirer to study the entry when he was called back: 'This isn't what I want. It's Noah's ark that I am interested in.'

Suitably chastened, the librarian started again. The *Micropaedia* had nothing relevant under 'ark', but under 'Noah' he found a brief reference to the ark, in which he and his family were saved from the flood, illustrated by a black-and-white photo of a 12th-century French fresco. More promising, among the cross-references to the *Macropaedia* was 'ark, legendary location', directing the reader to the article on Turkey, where there was a mention of 'Mt. Ararat, the highest peak in Turkey . . . the legendary site where Noah's ark came to rest'. With this answer the enquirer was obviously happier, but indicated that he would like more material. The other encyclopedias (*Chambers's, Collier's, World book*, etc.) confirmed Ararat as the place, *Americana* also citing the precise chapter and verse in the Bible – Genesis 8:4 – where Ararat is named as the site. Always worth consulting for biblical or historical topics, the 11th edition of *Britannica* (1910–11) referred to 'the tradition which makes Ararat the resting place of Noah's Ark', while leaving open the question of its historical authenticity. The article also mentioned a second site, Mount Judi in the south of Armenia: 'There so-called genuine relics of the ark were exhibited, and a monastery and mosque of commemoration were built; but the monastery was destroyed by lightning in AD 776, and the tradition has declined in credit.' Similarly discouraging was the newest encyclopedia, *Academic American/ Macmillan family*: 'Recent attempts to identify the ark's location at Mount Ararat are pseudoscientific and inconclusive. The most sensational evidence, a large wooden structure in northeast Turkey, has been scientifically dated as only 1,200 years old.'

Unable (even if willing) to dismiss the story of the ark as a complete legend – for it *may* have existed – the librarian realized that he was by this time almost certainly facing a research question, at least in the sense that the answer – one way or the other – had not yet been determined. Probably the most he could do for his enquirer would be to guide him to the current 'frontier of knowledge', in other words to trace for him the most recent research on the topic. By now the enquiry was bearing some of the signs suggesting that it might be suitable for an online search: a need for 'material on' the topic, i.e., bibliographical references in the first instance, combined with a requirement for the most up-to-date information; a manual alternative that would involve the routine checking of long runs of general periodical indexes (such as *British humanities index* and *Readers' guide to periodical literature*); the lack of specialized archaeology indexing and abstracting services in the library's collection (such as those in *Walford's guide to reference material: Annuario bibliografico di archaeologia, Archäologische Bibliographie* and *Bulletin signalétique: Art et archéologie*); and a very precisely defined and unambiguous topic.

But first it was necessary to select the appropriate database to search. A. T. Kruzas and J. Schmittroth, *Encyclopedia of information systems and services* (4th edition, 1981) had no entry for archaeology in its subject index, but the index to J. L. Hall and M. J. Brown, *Online bibliographic databases: a directory and*

16

sourcebook (3rd edition, 1983) directed him to FRANCIS (French Retrieval Automated Network for Current Information in Social and Human Sciences), a database 'with a substantial English language content' drawn from some 18 publications. The particular publication appropriate to this case appeared to be *Art and archaeology*. The huge listing by M. E. Williams, *Computer-readable databases: a directory and data sourcebook* (1982) confirmed FRANCIS as the only database to include archaeology. It added that the publication *Repertory of art and archaeology* was also covered, back to 1973, that in both cases the database contained the same number of references as the printed equivalents, and that of the journal articles included, 44 per cent and 23 per cent respectively were in English.

But then he encountered a check: FRANCIS was not available online from any of the online service suppliers for whom the library had a password (DIALOG, BLAISE and ESA/IRS). It was available only from Télésystèmes-QUESTEL based in Paris. Abandoning the idea of an online search he struck out in quite the opposite direction by consulting one of the reference librarian's most long-established and traditional printed 'databases', the vast array of *Notes and queries* volumes, well over 200 in number. Within seconds the cumulated indexes located for him in the issue for 5th October 1946 a brief article by M. Letts, 'The Ark on Mount Ararat', quoting from the accounts by writers from antiquity to the 19th century.

In the hope of more up-to-date articles of this kind the librarian asked his enquirer to help him check *British humanities index* and *Readers' guide to periodical literature* – neither of them at that time available online. Taking one each, and starting with the most recent issues, they worked backwards looking under both 'ark' and 'Noah' until they found something. *Readers' guide* was at first far more productive, with articles entitled 'Searching for Noah's Ark' (1983), 'Noah's Ark and biblical truth [expedition headed by J. Irwin]' (1982), indicating that the topic was still a live issue; by the time ten years had been searched some half-a-dozen more had been traced. All of course were in American journals, not all of which were available in the library, but the librarian chose to start with G. Gaskill, 'Mystery of Noah's Ark' in *Reader's digest* for September 1975, pages 150 to 154. Long experience had taught him that the articles cited thus in the American edition of *Reader's digest* could usually be traced in the British edition of the following month – as it proved again in this case. Captioned 'The hunt is keener than ever to solve Mount Ararat's 5,000 year old mystery', the article was located on pages 91 to 96 of the October 1975 issue, and described the author's visit to Ararat, prompted by a 1974 report that an orbiting US satellite had photographed an 'anomaly' that might be the ark. The extent of the bibliography on the topic was indicated by his assertion: 'I had a suitcase full of books, articles and newspaper clippings about people who thought they had found the ark.' Of course he did not find it either, and he concluded by quoting the Director of the University of Pennsylvania Museum: 'Absolutely anything is possible in this world, but if there is anything that's impossible in archaeology, this is it.'

British humanities index (and its predecessor, the Library Association *Subject index to periodicals*) had to be searched back to 1950 before anything was traced. In *Chambers's journal* for February of that year an article 'Noah's flood: can the ark be found on Ararat?' gave some account of the recent American expedition of Dr Aaron Smith, and in the same journal for June 1948 appeared an article describing some of the claims made over the years by people who had seen it, e.g., Russian and Australian airmen. The author's view at the time was that 'there seems to be no reasonable doubt that the Ark is still in existence and in fairly good condition'.

The mention by Gaskill of 'books' on the subject reminded the librarian that he had not consulted the bibliographies (though he had routinely checked the library catalogue without success). Not unexpectedly, he found in the *British national bibliography* several stories for children indexed under 'Noah's ark', and a number of references to the ark of Genesis, but he was genuinely surprised to encounter the specific subject heading 'expeditions to discover Noah's ark'. This led him to two books: T. F. Lattage and J. D. Morris, *The ark on Ararat* (1979), a 160-page abridged edition of a 1976 US publication, and R. Noorbergen, *The ark file* (1980), with 216 pages, originally published in the US in 1974.

This was the point at which the librarian indicated that he had taken the search far enough, and his enquirer accepted this, though he took up the offer to try to obtain the books just traced, opting for the larger and more recent of the two. When in due course it arrived, the librarian discovered that Noorbergen was an international journalist, and his volume a popular, even sensational, illustrated account of the 70 or so expeditions from the time of Aaron Smith to 1979, pointing out that 'none of them has ever returned with anything that even faintly resembles something that could have belonged to the ark'. In his introduction he quoted the opinion of an (unnamed) editor of a journal of exploration and discovery: 'If the ark of Noah is ever discovered, it will be the greatest archaeological find in human history.' Acknowledging that 'few other subjects are as controversial and debatable', he concluded optimistically that 'the overall developments are nevertheless encouraging enough to keep looking East'.

Some months later, by one of those chances which happen so frequently in reference work, and to which some have given the name 'reference hangover', the librarian noticed in his routine scanning of *The Times* a report from Ankara in the issue for 27th August 1984 that 'The leader of an American expedition said he was confident a boat-shaped formation found 5,000 ft up Mount Ararat in Eastern Turkey would prove to be Noah's Ark.' A photograph showed the president of the expedition, Marvin Steffins, posing with samples of rock and soil from the site. But he avoided making an official claim, would not venture a guess on the age of the samples, and said he was applying for a further expedition the following year.

'Curious questioners'

In sharp contrast to the researcher's lofty objective of pushing back the frontiers of knowledge, many an enquirer seems motivated by no more than 'mere' or 'idle' curiosity, as some librarians would term it. The burden of dealing with this kind of enquiry is one they feel uneasy under; their defensive stance was exemplified by one county librarian in his annual report when he explained: 'It would be quite wrong to think of the enquiry service as mainly a way of satisfying readers' idle curiosity.' Such librarians would no doubt agree with Milton when asked what God was doing before he made the world: somewhat testily he replied, 'He was making hell for curious questioners.' Yet others would argue that curiosity, one of the deep well-springs of human motivation, is to

19

be encouraged, not excused – particularly by a reference librarian, in whom a sharp intellectual curiosity is a *sine qua non*. Those who maintain this view are in good company: it was the great Dr Johnson who said, 'Curiosity is one of the permanent and certain characteristics of a vigorous intellect.'

People *are* curious, and libraries are for people. People do indeed turn to the printed word and to libraries to assuage their curiosity. The world's best-selling book is the *Guinness book of records*, a monument to human curiosity. The cartoonist R. L. Ripley's 'Believe it or not', aimed at a similar audience, became one of the most widely syndicated newspaper features in the world, appearing in 38 countries in 17 languages, as well as in book form, as radio programmes and film shorts; it has spawned at least half-a-dozen 'Believe it or not' museums, and is still going strong over 75 years after its first appearance.

Case 9: A question posed to a small reference library by telephone from an enquirer wanting to know what an eleven-sided figure was called in geometry seemed to the librarian to fall into the category that Sir John Betjeman once called 'footling facts'. Nevertheless, he felt he should try to help, and made his way to the scientific and technical dictionaries and encyclopedias. After a moment's thought he decided the appropriate heading to search was 'polygon'. He found that W. Karush, *The crescent dictionary of mathematics* (1962) only went as far as five sides, i.e., a pentagon. *Van Nostrand's scientific encyclopedia* (6th edition, 1983) gave the names right up to ten (decagon), and then simply stated 'etc.'. G. James, *Mathematics dictionary* (4th edition, 1976) did go beyond ten, but inexplicably jumped straight to twelve (dodecagon); *McGraw-Hill encyclopedia of science and technology* (5th edition, 1982) also went up to twelve, but skipped both nine and eleven.

The librarian decided that a radical rethink was needed. Recognizing that the terms used (like geometry itself, both the word and the science) derived from Greek, he turned to the language section. His knowledge of Greek was limited to an acquaintance with the Greek alphabet, which like the Russian alphabet he had taught himself in his few idle moments at the reference desk, so leaving aside for the moment what *Walford's guide* had told him was 'the indispensible classical Greek–English dictionary', H. G. Liddell and R. Scott, *A Greek–English lexicon* (9th edition, 1925–40), he looked for something much more elementary. He found it in F. K. Smith and T. W. Melluish, *Teach yourself Greek* (1947), where in the chapter devoted to numerals he found that the Greek for eleven (transliterated) was 'hendeca'. It was then but a matter of seconds to confirm from the *Concise Oxford dictionary* that a hendecagon was the name given to a 'plane figure with eleven sides and angles'.

Similar in some ways are the many quiz and competition queries that librarians particularly in public libraries are confronted with. Though the enquirers obviously do have a motivation beyond 'mere' curiosity this is usually no help to the librarian because the questions come devoid of context. Fortunately, almost invariably they are fact-finding queries, and for the experienced reference librarian they are usually simple to answer. They are also easy to spot, particularly when they come in convoy, as they often do. It is not unknown for the same question to be asked dozens of times in a single library within the space of a few days.

Case 10: 'What is "sphairistike"?' was the question over the phone from a caller who said she had tried her dictionary and encyclopedia without success. In response to his question she was able to spell the word for the librarian; her dictionary was the *Concise Oxford* and her encyclopedia was *Everyman's*. The librarian started his search with a quick check of his favourite dictionary, *Webster's third new international*, but drew a blank. He then tried his most recent desk dictionaries, *Chambers 20th century* (new edition, 1983), *Collins* (1979), and the new *Concise Oxford* (7th edition, 1982) – all to no avail. Finally he turned to the huge volumes of the *Oxford English dictionary* where he found that the word 'sphairistic', labelled '*rare*', meant tennis playing. The appended note told him that 'Lawn-tennis was first introduced in 1874 under the name *sphairistike*', derived from the Greek for 'playing at ball'.

Competition organizers often set their questions out of context deliberately, and sometimes word them to mislead. It is difficult to advise the young librarian how to spot these, but experience does develop a 'sixth sense'.

Case 11:   A request for the name of Noah's wife sent the librarian to the *Macmillan dictionary of women's biography* where he found that although there are entries (or cross-references) under a woman's married surname there are no cross-references from husbands' names as such. Turning to the universal biographical dictionaries he was somewhat surprised to find Noah ignored both by *Chambers' biographical dictionary* and *Webster's new biographical dictionary*. Even wider in scope, as its title indicates, is J. Thomas, *Universal pronouncing dictionary of biography and mythology* (*Lippincott's*), and here he did find ten lines on Noah, but no mention of a wife. It was a similar story in the *New century cyclopedia of names*: eight lines on Noah, but no reference to his wife.

Shifting his attention to specifically biblical sources he consulted J. Comay, *Who's who in the Old Testament* (1971) where Noah's wife was mentioned as accompanying her husband into the Ark, but was not named. Similarly unproductive was a search through J. Hastings, *A dictionary of the Bible* (in five volumes), *The interpreter's dictionary of the Bible* (in four volumes plus a supplement), and *The illustrated Bible dictionary* (in three volumes). Suspecting that he should have done so earlier, the librarian turned finally to the original source, locating precise chapter and verse by means of *Cruden's complete concordance to the Old and New Testaments*. Following up the two dozen references to Noah, he located in the book of Genesis the names of his father (Lamech), his three sons (Shem, Ham, Japheth), and five mentions of his 'wife' – but no name. He felt obliged to conclude that her name has not come down to us.

[This is the standard answer to this common enquiry, and the one usually regarded as 'correct' by competition setters and quiz questioners. But it is possible for a persistent reference librarian to take it one step further. In *Notes and queries* for 25th November 1909 the editor answered a correspondent thus: 'The name is not given in the Bible, but is added by later outside tradition as Waila.']

In this broad category too might be classed the hardy perennials – enquiries that library records show have been coming up regularly for years, indeed in some cases for generations: the vital statistics of the Venus de Milo; the gestation period of an elephant; the story of the willow-pattern plate; the origin and meaning of the words of the song 'Green grow the rushes, O'; how to go about leaving your body for medical research; how to make pot-pourri.

Case 12: Asked in a public reference library on what day of the week 4th August 1914 fell, the librarian recognized it at once as a very common type of enquiry, often asked by people about their date of birth. In this case, of course, the date had another significance in marking the start of World War I. Of the various ways to answer this question the librarian always favoured the encyclopedia. Under 'calendar, perpetual' in *New Britannica* (*Micropaedia*) she showed her enquirer the table with its clear instructions and helped him to use it – a matter of no more than a few seconds. The first step was to find from the top half of the table the proper dominical letter for the year in question: for 1914 this was D. Next it was necessary to find this same letter in the lower half of the table opposite to the month required, in this case August. Then they were able to read off the days of the week as appropriate: 4th August 1914 was a Tuesday.

Many enquirers approach librarians to help them settle an argument, commonly the subject of a bet into the bargain – and they will often be quite open about it. Their queries are usually about matters of simple fact and invariably require a precise and unambiguous answer. They frequently fall into that very large category of questions about the first, or the largest, or the fastest, or the highest, etc. – about records, in fact, of the *Guinness book of records* kind. It is interesting to recall that the genesis of the work, thirty years ago, was to provide 'a means for peaceful settling of arguments' of the kind common in pubs and bars. And of course Guinness is a firm of brewers.

However, as all experienced librarians know, the answers to some apparently straightforward questions of this kind are as much a matter of definition as of simple fact. This can require careful explanation to the waiting enquirer.

Case 13: 'What is the longest river in England?' was the simple phone query received one evening in a busy reference library. The librarian thought it must be the Thames, but as she knew she had to find documentary proof she quickly picked up the current *Whitaker's almanack*. Under 'rivers, longest' in the index she found the appropriate page number where after the world's longest rivers she found listed the Severn, 220 miles in length, and the Thames, 215 miles. 'It looks as if it is the Severn', she said, in surprise, 'but let me check somewhere else.' In the *Guinness book of records* she then read: 'The longest river in Great Britain is the Severn. . . . The longest river *wholly* in England is the Thames.' 'Of course', she said, 'the Severn starts in Wales.' She then explained to her somewhat befuddled enquirer that the simple definition 'longest river in England' was in fact ambiguous, logically including as it did rivers partly in England as well as rivers wholly in England.

Case 14: It took the librarian literally no more than a few seconds to find the capital of South Africa in the current *Statesman's yearbook*: at the head of the entry he read 'Capital: Pretoria'. But his caller was not satisfied: 'Are you sure it's not Bloemfontein?' Checking further, in *Whitaker's almanack*, he found in the section on South Africa under 'Capital': 'The administrative seat of the Government is Pretoria . . . the seat of the legislature is Cape Town.' But the caller still did not sound happy. Finally, the librarian brought *Information please almanac* to the phone and read out the following: 'Pretoria: administrative capital; Cape Town: legislative capital; Bloemfontein: judicial capital.'

The converse of the inadequately defined question is the one unwittingly phrased in terms too precise for the enquirer's real needs.

Case 15: A request as to whether Ray Milland was English or American might seem to the uninitiated a simple matter of fact, but the reference librarian had encountered difficulties in this area before and was well aware that he would have to discuss the matter further before beginning the search. His experience had taught him two things: nationality can be a very complex matter, even for those who are not international film stars. According to Reader's Digest *You and your rights: an A to Z guide to the law* (1980), 'Nationality has no legal definition in Britain . . . It generally has the same meaning as citizenship, but not always.' Secondly, he had learned that most people with such enquiries simply want to know where their man was born, not what citizenship he currently holds or what passport he carries. A few words with the enquirer established that this was so in this case also. Immediately *Who's who in America* provided the answer: 'b. Neath, Glamorganshire, Wales.' By birth, therefore, and in the general non-legal sense required by the enquirer, Ray Milland was seen to be neither English nor American, but Welsh.

There is no doubt that many of the problems posed to librarians appear trivial, scarcely warranting the expenditure of professional time, such as, 'Are there any words that rhyme with "orange"?' or 'What colour are French postboxes?' or 'Do horses have eyebrows?' Some public libraries refuse to answer quiz or competition questions as a matter of policy, and at least one textbook sternly advises: 'Discourage the trivial enquirer.'

This is dangerous counsel: the reference librarian should regard no enquiry as insignificant. In any case it is impossible to judge the importance of a query *merely from its subject matter*. Of course circumstances may dictate that not every question put in a library can receive the attention that in an ideal world the conscientious librarian would wish to give. But to discriminate between enquirers on the basis of the perceived triviality of their needs is to be avoided.

Case 16: When asked by telephone for the national flower of Finland the librarian immediately recalled a recent report in *The Times* about a librarian in a government library complaining bitterly at having to spend her professional time answering a trivial question of a very similar kind. But he had been better schooled and he set to with a will. He knew that a likely source would be the encyclopedias so he turned first to *New Britannica* where under 'Finland' he found the expected display 'box' giving a selection of key facts about the country, including a colour reproduction of the national flag – but not the national flower. At the head of the article 'Finland' in *Collier's* there was a similar summary, including the national anthem, the national holiday – but not the national flower. He did note, however, that at the head of the article on each state of the US (and each Canadian province) not only was the state flower listed but also the state bird, tree, fish, nickname, motto and song. *World book* under 'Finland' gave the national flag, national anthem, national coat of arms – but not the national flower.

Changing tack he started to look under 'flower'. He found nothing relevant in *Chambers's, Everyman's, Joy of knowledge/ Random House,* or *Academic American/Macmillan family*, but in *New Columbia* he read: 'Individual flowers . . . have become state flowers for many countries.' But the four examples given did not include Finland, and the article 'State flowers', to which reference was made, turned out to be devoted to the states of the US only. Finally in the index to *Americana*, his last hope, he found an entry 'flower: national flowers'. This proved to be a list of some 70 countries and their flowers: the national flower of Finland was given as the lily of the valley.

His enquirer was naturally pleased to have the answer when he called back, as he had been asked to. He then volunteered the information that his company were going to use the flower to help them make a favourable presentation to a Finnish company with whom they were negotiating an export deal.

The young reference librarian soon learns that some of the most trivial-seeming questions are dealt with seriously and often at some length in works of the highest scholarship.

Case 17: A request to know why the ends of table knives are rounded was plain enough, but the busy librarian had some difficulty at first in persuading himself to take it seriously. Recalling his duty, however, he thought he might as well try at least one or two encyclopedias. The index to *World book* led him to half a column under 'knife, fork, and spoon', but provided no further help. No explanation was found in *New Britannica* either, but the *Macropaedia* article on 'Cutlery and tableware' had a helpfully-annotated bibliography listing ten items of which the most promising seemed to be C. T. P. Bailey, *Knives and forks* (1927), 'a profusely illustrated treatise', and J. B. Himsworth, *The story of cutlery* (1953), 'a comprehensive account of the development and manufacture of various types'. As the enquirer seemed most anxious to pursue the matter the librarian arranged for copies of both these works to be supplied. The first to arrive, in due course, was the work by Himsworth, a Sheffield cutler, incredibly, for more than 70 years. Claimed by the publisher to be 'the first comprehensive history of the ancient craft of the cutler', it gave only one of its 14 chapters to table cutlery. There was no answer to the enquirer's question.

The second work was very different, by a different kind of author for a different audience. Compiled by a member of the staff of the Victoria and Albert Museum in London, it consisted mainly of full-page photographs (75 in all) of knives and forks from the Museum collection. Bailey's prefatory note said that 'there appears to be no monograph on the subject. The present work may, in fact, justly claim to be the first that has been written about knives and forks from the artistic or collector's point of view.' The scholarly accompanying text was no more than 15 pages, but it did at last satisfy the enquirer's curiosity. Until the end of the 16th century people carried food to their mouths with their fingers or with their knives, which were made pointed for that purpose. 'When the use of the fork became general the pointed knife was not needed for spiking the food, and from the latter part of the seventeenth century onwards we find most of the knives with rounded ends.' There was a story that Cardinal Richelieu had the points of all his knives ground down to discourage one of his regular but important guests from his habit of picking his teeth with the point of his knife. Better authenticated was the 1669 edict of Louis XIV, wishing to reduce the prevalence of assassinations at mealtimes, which made it illegal for anyone to carry pointed knives, for cutlers to make them, or for innkeepers to put them on their tables.

Readers' advisory work

It is possible to distinguish from reference work a special and very demanding kind of personal assistance to enquirers, usually known as readers' advisory work or reading guidance. The questions as put to the librarian might at first sight seem identical to material-finding enquiries of the 'Can you find me something on . . .?' type, but what the enquirer is seeking is guidance in the choice of suitable reading material rather than assistance in the search for information. The difference in such cases lies less in the nature of the topics asked about and more in the motives of the enquirers, which may not be obvious at the outset, even to the enquirers themselves.

Such motives can range from the simple cultivation of an interest to a desire to produce a change in oneself. What they have in common is that the enquirers have turned to reading as a means. It is obvious that needs of this kind cannot be satisfied on the instant, and thus on occasion the librarian has to be prepared to embark with the enquirer upon what might turn out to be a guided learning project extending over a period of weeks rather than a single information transaction. Equally obviously, the enquirer in such a case is seeking a book, or books, and usually wishes to take them away to read, rather than consult them on the spot. For such a reader the book represents encapsulated experience rather than a source of information.

It is clearly vital that such an enquiry is immediately perceived by the librarian not as a question to be looked up but as an expression of a personal concern that needs to be explored. The danger of course is that the librarian, naturally anxious to furnish an answer, may focus too narrowly on the subject of the question instead of the enquirer's need, which in such cases often requires teasing out.

Many, perhaps most, of the enquirers who approach librarians for this kind of help are 'adult independent learners', outside the formal education system. Research has revealed that a much greater proportion of adults than had once been thought are undertaking learning projects, mostly self-directed, informal, usually for practical reasons, and not aimed at academic credit. They may be acquiring or improving a skill, or seeking vocational advancement, or searching for understanding and even enlightenment. Many of them turn for assistance to books, and, in the words of Samuel Smiles, the great 19th-century apostle of self-help, begin 'reading to good purpose'. Among the many that librarians have assisted in their endeavours was the manual worker elected to office in his trade union who wished to learn more about politics and economics; the retired couple wanting to discover as much as possible about Spain in preparation for an extended visit; a group of nurses working with immigrant communities who wished to understand more about their patients' culture and home backgrounds.

Case 18: When asked in a busy city lending library for 'any books on franchising' the librarian felt it desirable to discuss the question a little further, partly to clarify his own rather vague ideas about the subject but also to ascertain more precisely the enquirer's need. For his part, the enquirer quite openly and happily explained that he had been obliged to take early retirement from his job, but that as his health and vigour were quite unimpaired he was seeking to go into business on his own account, using for the purpose the small capital sum he had recently received.

Pausing only to check the *Concise Oxford dictionary* definition of 'franchising' (in this sense 'Authorization to sell company's goods or services in a particular area'), the librarian consulted the catalogue. One book only was traced – M. Mendelsohn, *The guide to franchising* (3rd edition, 1982) – and it was missing from the shelf, presumably on loan. Turning therefore to the *British national bibliography* and searching backwards from the most recent issues he followed up the references under 'franchising:

Great Britain' in the subject index. (For the time being he decided to ignore 'franchising: United States', judging that legal and other differences between the two countries would probably make American books unnecessarily complicated for a beginner.)

Very quickly he located half-a-dozen titles. Setting aside for the moment those marked 'CIP [cataloguing in publication] entry', which are 'prepared from advance information supplied by the publisher and not from the book itself', he decided that the first was the most promising: G. Golzen, *Taking up a franchise* (1983). The second was Mendelsohn. The third, J. Adams, *Franchising: practice and precedents in business format franchising* (1981), the librarian judged to be a legal text. The fourth, S. Gunz, *Franchising* (1980), he felt safe in disregarding in this instance as it was described as a research report produced by the Manchester Business School and the Centre for Business Research.

Experience had taught him that a five-year search was normally adequate for such a topical business subject, so together with his enquirer they considered what to do next. It was decided to reserve the copy of Mendelsohn and the librarian agreed to recommend for purchase the modestly-priced Golzen. And for future reference he also drew his enquirer's attention to the citations for three other items that the search had revealed: two journals, *Franchise reporter* (1981–), eight times a year, and a quarterly, *Franchise world: business opportunities in franchise* (1978–); and *United Kingdom franchise directory* (1983–).

The first book to arrive was Golzen, a thoroughly practical paperback of 256 pages. Designed 'for anyone contemplating taking up a franchise', it was full of detailed advice, with half of its pages taken up by a guide in directory form to over a hundred 'Current franchise opportunities'. To judge from the titles of other books by the same author – *Changing your job, Jobs in a jobless world: where they are and how to get them, Working abroad, How to earn a second income* – he seemed well-qualified to advise, and to the librarian's experienced eye it seemed the ideal book for the purpose in hand.

In due course the work by Mendelsohn was returned from loan. Its 290 pages, written by a lawyer, appeared somewhat more thoughtful and objective; it was claimed to be 'for the franchisor and prospective franchisee alike'; on the practical side Chapter 13 was devoted to eight case studies of franchising in action. Though not a book to start with, the librarian judged it would add depth and perspective for his enquirer, once he had studied the book by Golzen.

The motives of other enquirers asking for advice about reading may be less immediately practical inasmuch as they may be seeking in a general way to widen their horizons or develop their awareness. They see reading as a means of growth. Examples taken from library records include the parents concerned that their growing children were outstripping them intellectually; the middle-aged secretary wishing to read and learn poetry, which she had previously been too busy to do; and the young man asking for books that would help him improve his conversational powers.

The librarian's response to readers' advisory enquiries can vary in formality of course, but commonly it appears as an individually prepared *list* of books, perhaps up to half-a-dozen in number, annotated and often with an indication of the order in which they might most profitably be read.

Over half a century ago it was very truly asserted that the necessary tools for a readers' adviser are brains and bibliographies. And indeed the reference work content is almost entirely bibliographical, using the standard apparatus familiar to all reference librarians, greatly enhanced over the last 50 years with a range of selective and evaluative bibliographies particularly useful in this kind of work. Obviously, the more extensive a librarian's first-hand knowledge of books, the more valuable will be the personal recommendations made, but there are always the bibliographies to fall back on. Where there is no substitute for brains is in the delicate process of fitting the book to the reader: what is required here is experience and a developed skill in interpersonal communication that allows the librarian within a short space of time to make a sympathetic and accurate assessment of the enquirer and of the enquirer's needs.

The emphasis in readers' advisory work on the book as experience does allow the librarian to recommend works of fiction in appropriate cases: enquirers interested in reading about the

French Revolution, for example, might find *The Scarlet Pimpernel* or *A tale of two cities* very much to their taste.

Case 19: 'Have you anything on mercenaries?' was the question posed by a young man in a busy college library. He agreed when the tutor-librarian asked if he meant soldiers who fought for pay and confessed that he had not tried to find anything for himself. Starting therefore with the encyclopedias, she found that *New Britannica* (*Micropaedia*) defined them as 'professional soldiers who fight for any state or nation without regard to national interests or issues'. She showed him the half-page in the *Macropaedia* and the column in *Chambers's*, but much of the text was historical, going back as far as ancient Egypt, and it soon became clear that it would not suit. Her enquirer made it plain he was hoping for 'books'. A quick check of the catalogue revealed two items, both found immediately on the shelf. The first was a 17-page pamphlet published by Her Majesty's Stationery Office in 1976: *Report of the Committee of Privy Councillors appointed to enquire into the recruitment of mercenaries*. The reader dismissed it with a glance. He expressed great interest in W. G. Burchett and D. Roebuck, *The whores of war: mercenaries today* (1977), a 240-page paperback, which the tutor-librarian left him to examine.

Within minutes he was back at the desk, his face registering considerable disappointment. 'Have you nothing else?' he said. Glancing quickly at the volume (a 'Pelican Original'), the tutor-librarian saw that the authors were an Australian freelance journalist and an English-born Professor of Law at an Australian university who had been asked to write the book by the International Commission of Inquiry on Mercenaries. It was a solid and serious work in which they claimed that they were trying 'to show how mercenaries are being used now', but she could well see how it lacked appeal for this particular enquirer. It took but a few moments further conversation to confirm what she had begun to suspect: her young enquirer had developed an enthusiasm for the subject – sparked off in fact by seeing the film *The mercenaries* on TV – and wanted to pursue it further. Clearly what would suit him best would be exciting accounts of modern mercenaries, preferably fighting in Africa, both fictional and non-fictional.

At this point she hesitated, aware that some of her colleagues were currently agitating in the professional journals for the banning from libraries of material of a 'warmongering and militaristic nature'. But then she also remembered that the published codes of professional ethics declared that librarians must resist all efforts by groups or individuals to censor library materials (American Library Association) and promote and protect the right of every individual to have free and equal access to sources of information without discrimination and within the limits of the law (Library Association).

Fairly sure that the college library had no further books on mercenaries she determined to press ahead and assist her enquirer with a brief list of titles which he would probably be able to obtain from the local public library. A check back through the subject index to the *British national bibliography* she judged the best way to start, and within minutes she had found several references. Passing swiftly over the books on mercenaries in ancient Iran and in the Byzantine Empire, German mercenaries in the War of American Independence, and various other inappropriate periods and locations, she used the very helpful *BNB* verbal feature headings to home in on J. Banks, *The wages of fear: the life of a modern mercenary* (1978) ('British mercenaries: autobiographies'); R. Steiner, *The last adventurer* (1978) ('German mercenaries: autobiographies'); C. Dempster, *Fire power* (1978) ('White mercenaries: Angola: officers' personal observations'); M. Hoare, *Congo mercenary* (1978) ('White mercenaries: Zaire: officers' personal observations').

BNB of course does not provide for access to fiction by subject, but in her search she had noticed title entries for half-a-dozen novels all called *The mercenaries* or *The mercenary*. This prompted her to turn to the *Fiction catalog* and its annual supplements, which does of course allow an approach by subject. The cross-reference in the title and subject index from 'mercenary soldiers' to 'soldiers of fortune' led her to F. Forsyth, *The dogs of war* (1974) which the helpful 13-line annotation made clear was set in an 'obscure West African republic'; W. Smith, *Cry wolf* (1976), about mercenaries in Tanganyika and Ethiopia fighting against Mussolini's Italian army in 1935; and D. E. Westlake, *Kahawa* (1982), set in contemporary Uganda. Curiously, C. Ozick, *A mercenary* (1976) appeared from its annotation not to be about mercenary soldiers at all.

A phone call to the local public library confirmed that they had copies of three of these fiction titles (not Westlake) and all of the non-fiction works and the tutor-librarian confidently referred her enquirer there.

The therapeutic value of books has been known for thousands of years; the Greeks regarded libraries as 'healing places of the soul'. A not inconsiderable number of those who come to librarians for reading guidance bring personal difficulties of one kind or another. These may range from vague feelings of dissatisfaction or personal inadequacy to a major life crisis, but in all such cases the enquirers are seeking to 'apply books to themselves' as a remedy. All too typical instances, sadly, taken from records kept by libraries, include the recently bereaved widow turning to books to while away the time, and the middle-aged man, unemployed for the first time in his life, anxious to occupy his mind.

Some librarians are apprehensive at the idea of treating readers with 'problems'; understandably they see clinical bibliotherapy as the province of the medical and ancillary professions. But many such 'problems' are normal stages of growth, basic tasks of living, life transitions which most individuals have to make – even though they may find them personally difficult. There is no doubt that reading can help: to the role played by the librarian in such instances some in the United States have given the name 'counselor librarianship'.

Case 20:   One busy evening in a small branch library of a city system a confident middle-aged woman asked for 'something on shyness'. The library catalogue had nothing on the subject, but the library assistant remembered the famous essay 'A defence of shyness' by Harold Nicolson reprinted in the Penguin *A book of English essays*. Quickly she found the volume on the shelf and re-read the opening words of the essay: 'It is surely discreditable, under the age of thirty, not to be shy. Self-assurance in the young betokens a lack of sensibility: the boy or girl who is not shy at twenty-two will at forty-two become a bore.'

While the enquirer was obviously grateful for this, she explained that what she really wanted was something for her son – 'one or two books that he could read that would give him advice'. As she was known as a regular library user, the assistant promised to let her have a list of recommended titles on her next visit. Consultation of the *British national bibliography* revealed a subject heading 'shyness: man: alleviation: manuals' which seemed tailor-made for this particular enquiry. Working backwards she first located M. Bentine, *The shy person's guide to life* (1984), but as this was a CIP entry and perhaps not yet published, she moved on. Next she found B. Powell, *Overcoming shyness: practical scripts for everyday encounters* (1979), originally published in Canada, and P. G. Zimbardo, *Shyness: what it is, what to do about it* (1977), originally published in the United States, and which she noticed had a 23-page bibliography. It seemed to her that half-a-dozen titles would be a sensible target to aim at, so she continued her search, noting another work of US origin, A. C. Wassmer, *Making contact* (1980), and two British titles, P. M. Shaw, *Shyness and anxiety* (1979), in the series 'Overcoming common problems', and C. H. Teear, *Conquer shyness* (1977). Then she consulted the invaluable *Public library catalog* and its annual supplements. The subject index under 'shyness' referred her to 'bashfulness', which in turn led her to entries for both Powell and Zimbardo. The 11-line annotation to the first, quoting *Publishers weekly*, described the work as a 'series of rehearsal scripts – practical exposures to stressful encounters . . . helpful in dealing with a problem said to affect more than 40% of our population'. The 10-line annotation for Zimbardo quoted from *Library journal*: 'The book presents many structural exercises . . . designed to relieve anxiety, build self-confidence, and gradually modify shy feelings and behaviors.'

With the possible exception of Wassmer, the assistant felt quite confident in suggesting these titles to her enquirer, accompanied by an offer to obtain one or more of them by purchase or inter-library loan.

Once again, the librarian's prescription need not be confined to didactic works; imaginative literature can play a particularly important role with such enquirers.

Another demanding yet very rewarding group of enquirers to serve are those who have caught 'the permanent habit of books' but have no particular subject in mind. Many public library users fall into this category, though most prefer to browse. Those that choose to approach the librarian either lack the time or inclination to select for themselves or, more commonly, are overwhelmed by the choice available and are eager for suggestions. What they seek are books that are 'good' or 'interesting', and preferably both. Typical examples noted by librarians include the enquirer seeking books to take away on her summer vacation, and the reader asking for something as different as possible from his work.

Similarly, not to be forgotten are those readers for whom the 'special reading experience' is sheer pleasure, to which they return again and again. Characteristic of this large group is the enquirer who had read all of Nevil Shute and wanted another similar writer. Perhaps most enquirers in search of recreational reading will expect the librarian to recommend fiction, but again the emphasis on the book as experience does not preclude appropriate non-fiction. Even when readers ask specifically for 'stories', for example, about Mississippi riverboats, or jungle survival, or South Wales coalminers, they may welcome books of personal reminiscences – which often tell a story as interesting as any novel. It would be an error to neglect such enquirers as less purposive than those pursuing a particular topic: the personal enrichment and raising of consciousness that a 'good' book can bring is not lightly to be disregarded.

Of course in such cases what is 'good' or 'interesting' so far as a particular reader is concerned is decided less on objective or abstract critical criteria and more by reference to the individual's own background, concerns and capacities, as ascertained by the librarian in discussion. And therein lies the art of readers' advisory work: not helping the enquirer to find 'a' book, but 'the' book – the one most suited at that particular time to that individual reader.

THE REFERENCE PROCESS

It is a serious error to think that reference work is simply a matter of answering questions. Experienced librarians can quote many examples of questions taken at their face value and answered in a perfectly adequate manner, but which still left the reader far from satisfied. It is far better thought of as problem-solving, with the actual identification of the reader's problem being just as important as hunting for the solution.

It is also a mistake to think there is a reference 'method' which can be applied in all cases where information is sought. Only in certain clearly defined fields is it possible to suggest a step-by-step line of approach in searching: some areas of chemistry, for example, or of law, are so fully documented that procedures for literature searches have been laid down with some success. This absence of a method does not mean that the librarian proceeds solely by inspiration, or even by rule-of-thumb. As Margaret Hutchins has said: 'Answering reference questions is a reasoning process . . . it should be thought through before a step is taken or a hand lifted towards a book.' It is possible, for example, to distinguish various stages in finding information for readers which in sum make up the reference process. It is true there are a very large number of variables in this process, and the stages frequently overlap. We must agree that it is by no means an exact science, but it *is* susceptible of a systematic approach.

Stage one: the reference interview

Just as the doctor's first task is diagnosis, the first stage of the reference process is determining the reader's problem, and this, as R. L. Collison reminds us, is 'half the battle'. The field over which this battle is fought is the 'reference interview', or as it is sometimes more aptly described, the 'reference encounter'. This is where the librarian must ensure, firstly, that there is no misunderstanding over the meaning of the question; secondly, that this question does in fact represent precisely what the reader wants;

and thirdly, that what the reader wants will in fact solve the problem. This is an area of professional endeavour demanding tact and patience, since the reader will only rarely provide all pertinent information without some prompting. The most common idiosyncrasy librarians have to prepare for is the request for material on a large subject when what is needed is a precise factual point within that subject. Enquirers will ask for 'the poetry books' when they want Chesterton's poem on courtesy, for Africa when they want *apartheid*, for books on pets when they want the quarantine regulations.

Case 21: 'I am looking for something on American elections' was the way the student in a south of England university library explained her need. Of course the librarian knew there were hundreds of books on the topic in the collection, so in the course of showing his enquirer the subject catalogue he asked her if there was any particular aspect she was interested in. Obviously somewhat overwhelmed by the mass of material revealed by the catalogue, she explained that it was really voting behaviour that she wanted to concentrate on. Closer scrutiny of the catalogue showed several appropriate titles, e.g., W. H. Flanigan, *Political behavior of the American electorate* (5th edition, 1983); G. C. Jacobson, *Strategy and choice in Congressional elections* (2nd edition, 1983); J. C. Pearce and J. L. Sullivan, *The electorate reconsidered* (1980). The librarian therefore decided he would now leave her to pursue the topic for herself.

Perhaps a quarter-of-an-hour later she was back at the desk, saying that she had still not found anything on precisely what she needed. 'Well, what *are* you looking for, exactly?' the librarian asked. Her reply was unhesitating: 'Something on ticket-splitting.'

Now it was out in the open, he felt much more confident of his ability to help, but he thought he should first get clear in his own mind what ticket-splitting was – for of course in Britain it is precluded by the system (at least in parliamentary elections) of voters having one vote to cast and one vote only. Ticket-splitting did not appear in the indexes to any of the American encyclopedias he consulted, and the references under 'voting' in *New Britannica, Collier's, Americana* and *Academic American/ Macmillan family* made no mention of it. But in *World book* he was directed from 'voting' to the article 'Ballot', where he read: 'The party column ballot [where candidates are listed according to party] makes it easier for voters to *vote a straight ticket* (vote for candidates of one party only). A ballot on which votes have been cast for candidates of different parties is called a *split ticket*.'

The library catalogue had no entry for ticket-splitting either, so the librarian took his enquirer to *Social sciences index*. Immediately an entry was found under 'ticket-splitting', referring the user to 'independent voting'. Searching backwards, they very quickly found four periodical articles with titles such as 'Ticket splitting and the vote for governor', 'In search of the ticket-splitter', etc., dating from 1980 to 1984. But then the trail grew cold: though they checked back as far as 1970, no more were found.

While his enquirer was noting the details, the librarian thought he would check the standard bibliographies of American books. Eventually, in *American book publishing record cumulative, 1950–1977* he traced (*via* the *Title index*, not the *Subject guide*) W. De Vries and L. Tarrance, *The ticket-splitter: a new force in American politics* (1972), a work of 149 pages, which, he saw, 'includes bibliographical references'. As the library had no copy he offered to try to obtain it on interlibrary loan.

Before leaving her he made sure she knew how to track down the periodical articles she had made a note of. Taking as an example the most recent, they located it in the May 1984 issue of *Professional geographer*, the journal of the Association of American Geographers. The six-page article, rather technical in content, was 'The geography of ticket-splitting', and was in fact by two British scholars, R. J. Johnston and A. M. Hay of the University of Sheffield. The abstract began: 'Ticket-splitting is becoming increasingly common in American national elections, according to the results of voter surveys.'

As the last case would suggest, librarians' instant recognition that they are totally ignorant on the topic asked about by no means unfits them to provide real assistance to the questioner. A genuine admission of the fact will often call forth sufficient explanation from the enquirer to set the librarian on the right track. Where this does not suffice consultation of a dictionary or encyclopedia usually provides a remedy.

Case 22: 'Can you tell me what a pomander was used for?' was the question asked in a small public library. Wisely acknowledging her mystification, the librarian first asked her enquirer 'Do you know how you spell it?' and then 'What is it like?' All the enquirer was able to add was that it was some kind of small ornament or decorative object. Remembering the advice given her at library school that the encyclopedia is the place to start when you can't think of a place to start, the librarian consulted *New Britannica*. Under 'pomander' in the *Micropaedia* she found 16 lines about this 'small metal (sometimes china) container designed to hold a ball of aromatic spices or herbs. Worn suspended from neck or girdle or attached to the finger by a ring, it was believed to be a protection against infections and noxious smells.' The article was illustrated by a detail from a 1453 portrait by Cranach the Younger showing a pomander being worn on a chain round a man's neck.

A not uncommon hazard at this stage of the reference interview is simple mishearing. Repeating or even paraphrasing the enquirer's question is a standard interviewing technique to be used here, and will usually serve to distinguish an enquiry about 'glovemaking' from one about 'lovemaking', or 'Jesus' from 'cheeses'. What it may not do is differentiate *'Red shoes'* from 'Reg Hughes', or 'salt' from 'SALT' [Strategic Arms Limitation Talks].

Case 23: When asked 'Have you got anything about Eleanor Crosses?' the librarian responded by enquiring, reasonably enough, 'Do you know whether she is still living or not?' He was surprised to find that this caused some amusement, the reason for which became plain when the enquirer gently explained that they were actually memorial crosses to Queen Eleanor. Now wiser, the librarian soon picked out from the four Queen Eleanors in *New Britannica* the appropriate Eleanor of Castile, queen consort of Edward I of England. The short entry concluded: 'Upon her death [in 1290 at Harby, Nottinghamshire], Edward erected the famous Eleanor Crosses – several of which still stand – at each place where her coffin rested on its way to London.' *Everyman's* and *Joy of knowledge/Random House* carried similar information, though omitting to state that some crosses were still extant. The largest British encylopedia, *Chambers's*, as expected for a historical query of this type, was the most informative of all with an 11-line paragraph in the two-page article 'Crosses'. The librarian read that 'Three of these remain, at Hardingstone near Northampton, at Waltham and, of somewhat different design, at Geddington near Kettering'. A small black-and-white line drawing of the first accompanied the text. Further, 'A modern repro-duction in the yard of Charing Cross [London] railway station marks the site of one removed by order of Parliament in 1647.'

In the hope of a photograph the librarian turned finally to the most lavishly illustrated British set, *New Caxton*, where he was rewarded with a fine clear coloured photograph of the cross at Geddington. The text added that, 'In folklore the best known of these crosses was at Banbury. The last of them was at Charing, between the City and Westminster Abbey.'

[Strangely, there is one important detail that none of the British encyclopedias give, though *Americana* does: Edward built 12 crosses in all.]

Enquiries without precise answers
One minor irritant it is well to be forewarned about: even after refining at the reference interview stage, many questions (particu-larly if they involve statistics) remain unsatisfactory in that they are not susceptible of the straight answer so frequently expected.

Case 24: At first the request received in a west of England city library for the population of Rome about the year 100 BC seemed quite simple. Even from his slight knowledge of ancient history the librarian felt sure that the highly efficient Romans would have collected such statistics. And so it proved: the *Oxford classical dictionary* (2nd edition, 1970) article on 'population (Roman world)' informed him that 'The republican period has left thirty-seven census figures which, although derived from a number of different authors, are sufficiently self-consistent to appear authentic for the most part.' The years nearest to 100 BC for which figures appeared were 115/14 BC: 394,336 and 86/5 BC: 463,000.

So far so good, but the librarian felt obliged to point out two uncomfortable facts made clear in the article. Firstly, 'the census was not always a thorough record of actual citizen numbers'; and secondly, in any case censuses at that period were confined to 'adult male citizens', thus excluding for example children, women and slaves.

Case 25: When asked in a college library for the population of Nigeria the librarian reached confidently for *Whitaker's almanack* where he found that the 1963 census figure was 55,654,000. As this was more than 20 years earlier he was relieved to see a note that 'U.N. estimates of the present population suggest a figure of 85 million'. His enquirer found this wording somewhat vague, so he turned to *New Encyclopaedia Britannica* (1983 printing). In the *Macropaedia* article on Nigeria he found similar figures (1980 estimate 84,731,600; 1963 census 55,670,100) together with another note: 'Both the 1963 census and the 1980 estimate may be overstated.'

He knew that the 'Addenda' in the *Micropaedia* also contained statistics so he consulted the appropriate table, where he found a later census figure, for 1973: 79,760,000. But once more he found a note, 'possible overenumeration; compare 1977 estimate'. This estimate he found to be 78,790,800. By now he was thoroughly confused, so he turned to the *Statesman's year-book*. There he read: 'The results of the 1973 census were abandoned in Aug. 1975 because they "will not command general acceptance throughout the country". There is considerable uncertainty over the total population, but one estimate based on electoral registration in 1978 is 95m. and the World Bank give an estimate of 81,039,000.'

Young librarians soon learn, however, that even in cases where there is no precise answer to the enquirers' questions, it is usually possible to make a response that they find adequate. Sometimes this can be no more than a courteous demonstration of the reason for the absence of an answer, but surprisingly often the librarian is able to come up with something of relevance which satisfies the enquirer, even though it may not be the answer originally sought.

Case 26: When asked in the reference library of a north country seaside town for the names of the Knights of the Round Table the librarian suspected his task might not be as simple as it sounded. He was not quite sure where to start for one thing: he knew that there was some historical evidence for the existence of Arthur, but that most of the stories associated with him and his court are legends. After a moment's thought he made first for the three-volume *New century cyclopedia of names*, which he knew gave 'essential facts about more than 100,000 proper names of every description'. The entry under 'Round Table' made quite clear that it was legendary, and added confusingly, 'The table would seat 150 knights. (In some accounts it would seat 1600, in others only 50 or 13).' More interesting, to both librarian and enquirer, was the statement that followed: 'There is a round wooden board hanging in Winchester Castle, depicting the figure of Arthur and showing the names of 24 knights, which is traditionally said to be the original.' *Brewer's dictionary of phrase and fable* informed them that 'The table shown at Winchester was recognized as ancient in the time of Henry III [1207–72] but its anterior history is unknown. It was for the accommodation of 12 favourite knights.'

The librarian and his enquirer then paused to confer. They decided that their best course was to find an illustration of the actual Winchester table, genuine or not, in order to see what were the names shown, whether 24 or 12. A glance at the catalogue soon revealed a number of books on the Arthurian legend, and within minutes the desired illustration was found in G. Ashe, *The quest for Arthur's Britain* (1968) in the shape of a full-page photograph of the table. As described, Arthur was depicted enthroned, and round the edge of the table in large gothic letters – very difficult to read – were the names of 24 knights, starting on the king's left hand, the Siege Perilous, with Sir Galahallt, and then Sir Lancelot deu Lake, Sir Gaven, Sir Percivale and all the rest.

There are occasions of course when it can be more difficult to convince enquirers that matters are not always as precise or as clear-cut as they would wish.

Case 27: The student in a college library seeking to discover what constitutes a 'breach of the peace' seemed by his manner to have a more than academic interest in the matter and the librarian naturally was inclined to treat the enquirer as sympathetically as possible, though well aware of the pitfalls of attempting legal advice. She judged that finding a simple definition would be a legitimate task for her to undertake, and so she turned to *Osborne's concise law dictionary* (6th edition, 1976). There she was puzzled to find a ten-line entry that seemed not to define the phrase, which can relate to 'apparently any crime or offence whatever'. *Stone's justices' manual* had several references to breach of peace but none with a simple explanation. Feeling she was already in deep water she retreated in the direction of the layman's guides that she had used in the past. *Everyman's own lawyer* disappointed her, lacking any reference in the index, either under 'breach' or 'peace', but Reader's Digest *You and your rights: an A to Z guide to the law* informed her of what she was beginning to suspect: 'There is no precise definition of what constitutes a breach of the peace.'

This was clearly not to her enquirer's taste, though she did point out the paragraphs explaining that 'it is generally taken to mean the use, or the threat, of force against someone, or behaviour which causes someone reasonably to apprehend danger'.

The unforthcoming enquirer
Enquirers do not of course deliberately conceal information from the librarian they ask to help them. Occasionally a secretive reader is encountered, but more often than not facts are withheld simply

because the modest reader, like the witness in a court case, does not appreciate the potential value of what may seem to be very minor details or clues. One of the major advantages the trained reference librarian has over the non-professional is a greater awareness that practically any question can be approached from more than one angle. This advantage can be thrown away unless all pertinent information is extracted from the reader at the outset.

Case 28: Obviously the catalogue was the first place to start with an enquiry as to whether the reference library had any books on the Macaulay system of shorthand. There was nothing relevant under Macaulay (or Macauley) in the name sequence, and although the classified sequence showed a surprising number of books on shorthand – mostly on the Pitman or Gregg systems, but also on Beers, Dewey, Dutton, Fishwick, Gurney, Lightning, Notehand, Thomas, Yatrol and many others – nowhere was Macaulay mentioned.

'I am sorry, we don't seem to have anything on it at all' was the librarian's over-hasty reply. 'It's a very old system – not used at all now', the enquirer volunteered. Of course, as the librarian realized with more than a touch of guilt, this put an entirely different complexion on the matter. She had noticed three or four books in the catalogue on the history of shorthand, of which the most promising were E. H. Butler, *The story of British shorthand* (1951) and I. Pitman, *A history of shorthand* (undated). Taking a chance on Macaulay being British, she turned first to Butler, where immediately she found four index references to Aulay Macaulay. A Manchester tea merchant, he had published his own system in 1747 as *Polygraphy; or shorthand made easy to the meanest capacity*, which Butler described as 'a neat little volume, handsomely bound and beautifully printed from engraved plates'. But he gave little information about the system itself.

The library's copy of Pitman was found to be the fourth edition, which from internal evidence the librarian was able to date approximately to 1917. Describing itself as 'mainly a history of English shorthand systems', it had only one index reference to 'Macaulay' (no first name or initials). This led to some 16 lines on page 41, confirming Butler, and adding, 'This is a very inefficient system, and could never have been written for any length of time by anyone but the author himself.' Glancing through the volume the librarian noticed an appendix (unindexed), 'Table of English stenographic alphabets' covering 1602 to 1882, in which 'Macaulay 1747' had a column to himself, giving his equivalents for the 26 letters of the alphabet and for 'ch', 'sh' and 'th'.

It is often equally difficult to ascertain the level, form and amount of material required, but obviously it is equally important for success. More often than not this involves an assessment of the capabilities of the reader, which must be made during the reference interview. This usually necessitates finding out what the reader already knows and what sources (if any) have already been tried.

Case 29:   It was obvious that the enquirer in a polytechnic library seeking books on football would have to be questioned further. For a start, it would need to be established whether 'football' meant association football ('soccer') – as was most likely – rugby football, or even American football. The librarian also knew that the overwhelming majority of books on football were popular in character, comprising biographies of players, illustrated annuals, quiz books, compilations of records, 'how-to-play' manuals, etc., none of which were likely to be found in an academic library. For an investigator wishing to make a serious study of this kind of literature the best source would be a copyright deposit library.

The enquirer was quite happy to explain that he was a sociologist interested in football – by which he meant soccer – as a social phenomenon. He knew that there had been several academic studies in recent years and he wanted help in tracing them. The library catalogue revealed only two works: the first, a government pamphlet, was the *Report of the Working Group on football crowd behaviour* (1977); the enquirer noted the call number but said he was much more interested in the second, which he proposed to borrow. This was J. Walvin, *The people's game: a social history of British football* (1975). Both librarian and enquirer saw with interest the note in the catalogue to the effect that the work had a seven-page bibliography. The librarian promised to search for any studies more recent than 1975.

Clearly the most useful bibliography to consult was the *British national bibliography*, excellent for this kind of subject approach. He began his search with the 1975 volume, and immediately under 'football' he was presented with the three possibilities: American, association, rugby. He soon picked out the relevant entry, 'association football: Great Britain: social aspects: to 1974', which led him to Walvin's book. Working his way forward he soon found the 1977 Working Group report, and then another official report, from the Sports Council, E. Dunning, *Soccer: the social origins of the sport and its development as a spectacle and a profession* (1979). He continued his search down to 1984, finding two works on English football, A. Mason, *Association football and English society, 1863–1915* (1980) and S. Wagg, *The football world* (1983) – a CIP [cataloguing-in-publication] entry for a book not yet published; and then under the sub-heading 'anthropological perspectives', D. Morris, *The soccer tribe* (1981); and under 'Brazil: sociological perspectives', J. Lever, *Soccer madness* (1983). He rang his enquirer with the details, offering to obtain the works on interlibrary loan.

He made a point of examining Walvin when it was returned. He saw with interest that it described itself as 'the first attempt to consider the history of football within British society', and that it was based on a series of lectures delivered at the University of York, where the author was a member of the history department. The librarian was encouraged to read in the acknowledgements that 'David Griffiths of the University of York Library helped me more than any other person, indefatigably supplying me with obscure references, leads and provocative ideas.'

He also noted that the 150-item bibliography included a number of university theses (including, rather surprisingly, a PhD from Ohio State). This prompted him to check the *ASLIB index to theses*, where he soon located a number of titles of which the most promising appeared to be a Birmingham 1982–3 MPhil, K. Fradley, *Football hooliganism demystified: an examination of football crowd disorder in the West Midlands*; and a Leicester 1977 MPhil, S. E. Wagg (a name he had already encountered), *Well, Brian: a sociological study of the professional football community.*

47

Once more he phoned his enquirer, and explained how to go about obtaining these theses.

Case 30: The elderly enquirer in a large city reference library explained that he was seeking illustrations of an old-fashioned blacksmith's shop to use in a talk he had been asked to give at a local college. From the catalogue the librarian suggested two likely books: C. McRaven, *Country blacksmithing* (1981), which the subtitle said contained photographs and drawings, and *Read about blacksmith's shops* (1975), with 'Col. ill.'. The latter was a 32-page pamphlet, with a coloured photograph at virtually every opening – though not all of them were about a blacksmith's work. The former was an American work, 'a complete step-by-step guide to working with iron', illustrated with over 200 black-and-white photographs and drawings.

While the enquirer was studying these with obvious interest, it crossed the librarian's mind that there might well be material available on film that could be used to illustrate a talk. The obvious source to check was the microfiche *British universities film and video catalogue*, the index of which led him to a 28-minute colour video cassette, *Blacksmiths of Chatham Dockyard* (1983), available on special loan (or sale) from the National Maritime Museum. The librarian showed his enquirer the annotation: 'An archival record . . . showing a number of craft skills. . . . The narrator was chief foreman of the shop.' Consultation of the *British catalogue of audiovisual materials* (1979) and *Supplements* (1980 and 1983) revealed a 16mm colour film, *The blacksmith* (1978), running for 11 minutes, showing 'a modern blacksmith at work and examples of his craft'. The hire fee quoted was £5.50. Both of these suggestions were received with enthusiasm.

Case 31: In a small further education college library a student approached the tutor-librarian for help with his project on the history of the chisel. From experience the tutor-librarian knew that some of projects set to the students were quite extensive, often contributing a large share to their overall assessment at the end of the course. But she suspected that in this instance that was not the case. A few moments' discussion made clear that he was a craft student on a carpentry course who had been asked by his lecturer in communications to write something for reading out at the next class meeting.

As the library catalogue had nothing specific under 'chisels', the tutor-librarian quite sensibly thought that encyclopedia articles might suffice. The entries in *Everyman's* and *World book* had nothing historical at all, but *New Britannica* was far more informative. The nine-line *Micropaedia* told them that 'Flint ancestors of today's chisel existed as far back as 8000 BC; the Egyptians used copper and later bronze chisels.' Of the four references to the *Macropaedia* the most useful was to a 20-page article 'Hand tools', which included five paragraphs on the history of the chisel.

Though the student sat down quite contentedly with the volume the tutor-librarian thought he could probably use a little more. She had noted, in the useful annotated bibliography appended to the article, W. L. Goodman, *The history of woodworking tools* (1964), described as 'definitive and comes up to the present'. Examining the library's copy she learned that its contents had first appeared as a series of articles in *Practical education*, the journal of the Institute of Handicraft Teachers. On 'chisels and gouges' there were only three-and-a-half pages, compared to 50 pages on the saw, but she judged that this would be just right for her enquirer.

The enquirer's motives

It is often useful to know the purpose for which the enquirer needs the information. Tact is required if the librarian judges it necessary to ask for this directly, but some will volunteer the information and many will be willing to explain if required.

Case 32: In search of a large coloured picture of a Chinese dragon the librarian was already on her way to the shelves when her enquirer called after her, adding to his original request, 'I would like it to be in the authentic colours.' Inevitably this made her pause: surely the dragon was a mythical beast? What could 'authentic' mean in such a context?

When she asked him, he admitted he was not sure, but went

on to add, 'It's for tattooing.' Privately she felt grateful that the reason for his request was none of her business, but she did realize that now she had been made aware of it, she was indeed clearer in her own mind what she was looking for – a genuine Chinese coloured reproduction, preferably ancient – and thus 'authentic'. She recalled a curious book called *The dragon* in the collection somewhere, and the title entry in the catalogue soon enabled her to track it down, written by C. Gould and published in 1977. She found that pages 63 to 79 were devoted to 'The Chinese dragon'; she read that China is 'a country in which the belief in the existence of the dragon is thoroughly woven into the life of the whole nation'; there were half-a-dozen illustrations, but all were black-and-white.

Her attempted short cut having thus led nowhere, she returned to the conventional path and consulted J. C. Ellis, *Index to illustrations* and the various editions of the *Illustration index*. In the first, under 'dragon, snakes (China town parade)' she found a reference to a coloured illustration in the *National geographic magazine* for August 1956. She had of course used this periodical many times before, and knew it as one of the best sources of illustrations in the library. She was therefore not surprised to find two further references to it in *Illustration index* under 'dragons: China (150 B.C.)' and 'dragons: embroidered badge (China)', directing her to the issues for May 1974 and January 1974 respectively, with coloured illustrations being indicated in both cases.

As she expected, the first of these proved to be a photograph of the celebrations in San Francisco's Chinatown, showing the 100-foot monster, specially imported from Canton, snaking through the 'Street of a Thousand Lanterns', together with a second photograph showing a close-up of the head. Neither was at all satisfactory for her enquirer's purpose. The May 1974 illustrations were much more helpful, comprising photographs of a seven-foot silk banner recently recovered from a Han dynasty tomb of 2,100 years ago, showing several winged dragons – obviously authentic.

But the last photograph, of an embroidered badge for a formal robe of the Ming dynasty, seemed the best of all. Reproduced in splendid colour, actual size, on a fold-out page, it was, as the caption truly described it, 'breathtaking'. The enquirer was not impressed: 'That's not a dragon', he said. The librarian looked again. Sure enough, splendid though it was, the beast had no wings. She read the accompanying text, where she saw that it was described as a lion. She found herself apologizing for the error in *Illustration index*, but her enquirer assured her he was more than happy with his Han dynasty dragons.

It is bad practice, however, for the librarian to ask why the information is needed unless it would help in understanding the enquirer's need or would facilitate the subsequent search. Provided the question is clear the librarian should refrain from asking out of curiosity, however tempting it may be to explore the reasons behind some of the extraordinary questions that library users ask.

Case 33: A question asked one morning in a college library a hundred miles away from the nearest sea was, 'Who owns a whale washed up on the beach?' Suppressing her natural curiosity, all the librarian said was, 'That's probably a legal question but I'll see what I can find.' She then tried her regular standby in such cases, *Everyman's own lawyer*. The index had no entries under either 'beach' or 'whale', so she was just about to try 'fish' when she recalled that the whale is in fact a mammal. Though there was nothing under 'mammal' there was an entry 'animals – whales'. This led her to the plain statement that whales are 'royal fish' and 'if the property in them is not otherwise definable, [they] belong, when within the British Dominions, to the Queen by virtue of her prerogative'. A footnote added, 'It is Her Majesty's intention shortly to give up her prerogative right to whales.' The librarian pointed out to her enquirer that the edition she had used was dated 1981 and added the usual advice to check with a lawyer to be absolutely sure about the current position.

[What a lawyer (or indeed a law librarian) might do to check would be to consult *Halsbury's Laws of England* together with its elaborate supplementary apparatus for keeping up to date. The interim index to the currently appearing 4th edition covers volumes 1 to 42 only, but under 'whale: ownership of – territorial waters' the user is directed to volume 18, para 917 where appears confirmation that 'All whales taken within the territorial waters of the kingdom or stranded on the shore are treated as royal fish and belong to the Sovereign in right of the crown.'

As the date of the volume is 1977, in order to determine whether the legal position has since changed it is necessary to consult first the latest annual *Cumulative supplement*, looking under the same reference as in the main set, i.e., volume 18, para 917. Secondly, it is necessary to consult the looseleaf *Current service*, checking again under volume 18, para 917 in the 'Key' to see whether either the *Monthly reviews* or the accompanying 'Noter-up' shows any change later than the *Cumulative supplement*. No change had been noted in either up to September 1984.]

Case 34: 'What are the orders of angels?' asked in a London borough library was a question the librarian did not quite understand at first, but his enquirer helpfully explained that they were like ranks, in the army, for example. He soon found fuller details in *New Britannica* under 'angels, hierarchy of' in the *Micropaedia*: 'an order or ranking of celestial or spiritual beings or entities in Western religions'. The number of such rankings was often four, seven, or twelve. Details were given of those in Zoroastrianism, Judaism and Islam, but the enquirer indicated that it was Christianity he was interested in and therefore sat down to copy out the nine orders given: angels, archangels, seraphim, cherubim, virtues, powers, principalities, dominions and thrones.

Within a few moments he returned to the desk with an important question: 'Which of these is the highest?' After scanning the article again to confirm that it was indeed silent on the point, the librarian turned to *World book*, where he read: 'Seraphim rank highest, followed by cherubim, thrones, dominions, virtues, powers, principalities, archangels and angels.' But this was obviously in an order significantly different from the *New Britannica* list, which perhaps was not intended to be arranged by rank at all. A third encyclopedia, *Academic American/Macmillan family*, confirmed *World book*, though listing them in reverse order, i.e., beginning with the lowest. At this point the librarian quietly withdrew.

Of course it does sometimes happen that the librarian's approach is dictated by the form in which the enquiry is received. A question asked by letter obviously eliminates the reference interview, and the librarian is occasionally obliged to adopt the posture of a mind reader.

Case 35: A typewritten letter received in a north of England reference library simply asked whether 'any other countries have the same national anthem as us'. After consulting colleagues the librarian decided that her enquirer was probably thinking about the tune rather than the words; indeed one of her colleagues was sure that Americans also used the tune. Unsure at first where to begin, she decided to try the encyclopedias. Under 'national anthem' in *New Britannica* she discovered firstly that 'The oldest national anthem is Great Britain's "God Save the Queen" ', and secondly, that though some are written specifically others are 'adapted from existing tunes'. For example, the German national anthem before 1922 was sung to the melody of 'God Save the Queen', as is the United States unofficial anthem 'America', or 'My country 'tis of thee'. *Collier's* immediately seemed to contradict this in part: 'The oldest anthem sung today, the Netherlands' *William of Nassau*, dates from about 1626.' It did concede, however, that 'God Save the Queen' of 1745 was the runner-up, and also confirmed the enquirer's suspicion that 'anthems of nations far from . . . Great Britain emulate . . . *God Save the Queen*'. The article listed over 120, but the only countries noted as using 'God Save the Queen' were certain British Commonwealth countries, which the librarian felt did not count. Most unusually for *Collier's*, which collects all its bibliographies in its final volume, there was a reference to P. A. Scholes, *God save the queen* (1954) in the body of the article.

The largest British encyclopedia, *Chambers's*, had surprisingly nothing at all to offer, but *Everyman's* added Switzerland and Denmark to Germany and the United States as countries that had adopted (and adapted) the tune, and also noted Scholes.

The library had a copy of this work, subtitled *the history and romance of the world's first national anthem*. A typically idiosyncratic work by the author of the *Oxford companion to music*, it was nevertheless thoroughly scholarly, the result of vast research extending over several years and many continents, and a product of the Oxford University Press. The librarian was able to quote for her enquirer the statement at the beginning that 'at one time or another about twenty countries on the Continent of Europe, adapting to it their own sets of words, have borrowed it, making it their own "National Anthem" '. She also added in her reply that Chapter 21 was called 'Continental adoption of the British tune', and Chapter 22 was 'The tune in America'.

Librarians have often speculated on the reasons behind the enquiries that they receive. Apart from the more obvious circumstances such as the need to know for a practical purpose, or in connection with a course of study, formal or informal, or just general interest in a subject, enquirers often simply seek elucidation of some half-understood allusion to a topic that they have heard about in conversation or seen on television or come across in their reading. Students commonly ask about matters they have heard mentioned in lectures but have been unable or reluctant to ask the speaker about.

Case 36: The student asking in a busy public library about the riddle of the sphinx had encountered it in his reading, but had not found any further explanation. He had tried the encyclopedias in his college library without success. When the librarian probed a little further to see if he had found anything he said he had found the riddle mentioned in *Britannica*, though it had not answered his question, and he had found the sphinx mentioned in *Chambers's*, but not the riddle.

Tactfully the librarian asked if he would mind her just checking again, and she soon found the one-and-a-half column *Micropaedia* entry in *New Britannica* under 'Sphinx'. There was a black-and-white photo of the most famous, the Great Sphinx at Giza in Egypt, but no more than a reference to the riddle: 'The Sphinx is famous in Greek legend as an omniscient being who posed a riddle that no man but Oedipus could answer.' Annoyingly the riddle itself was not given. Turning to *Chambers's* the librarian consulted the index first (which she suspected her enquirer had not done). The first of the two references she found directed her to the main article under 'sphinx' that the student had already seen, and true enough there was no reference to a riddle though it did make an important distinction: 'It cannot be too strongly stressed that the Greek sphinx has nothing in common with the Egyptian.' But the second reference was to the article 'Oedipus' which her enquirer had missed, and though it did not resolve his problem it did add some circumstantial detail: 'When he came to Thebes he found the city plagued by a monster, the Sphinx or Phix, which devoured men if they could not answer a riddle she propounded; he solved it and she killed herself in disgust.'

The distinction between the Greek and the Egyptian sphinxes proved helpful when they consulted *Collier's encyclopedia*. The index furnished six references under 'sphinx (Egy.)' which they felt they could safely ignore, while concentrating on the five references under 'sphinx (Gr. myth.)', and in particular the one which appeared also under 'sphinx (leg.)'. This led directly to the article 'Monsters and mythical beasts', containing a quarter-page photograph of the Greek sphinx – quite different in appearance from the more famous sphinx of Egypt – with the caption: 'The Greek sphinx throttled all passers by who could not solve her riddle: "Who walks on four legs in the morning, on two at noon, and on three in the evening?" The hero Oedipus finally gave the correct answer – it is a man, who crawls as a baby, walks upright as a man, and leans on a cane in old age.' Double checking, as is always advisable with encyclopedias, the librarian found that *World book encyclopedia* confirmed this, and added a dramatic tailpiece: 'The Sphinx became furious because Oedipus had given the right answer. She howled with rage and finally threw herself from the rock [outside the city of Thebes on which she lived] to her death.'

[A shorter route to the same answer would have been *Brewer's dictionary of phrase and fable* under 'sphinx'.]

Case 37: 'I came across a reference to Robert Montgomery the other day. He was described as a poet who "injured not poetry but himself". Who was he exactly? I can't find him in any anthologies.' The librarian's sensible response to this clearly stated enquiry was to ask where the reader had seen the reference. 'Oh, it was in the introduction to a 'World's Classics' book of detective stories' was the precise, but in the event not particularly helpful, reply.

Montgomery was unknown to the *Poets* volume in the 'Great writers of the English language' series, so the librarian tried the time-saving *Index to the Wilson author series* (1976), which directed her at once to S. J. Kunitz and H. Haycraft, *British authors of the 19th century* (1936). There she found three-quarters of a column on this 'illegitimate son of a school-mistress by a well-known clown named Robert Gomery'. He added the prefix 'Mont' to make his name sound more aristocratic. Writing mainly religious verse, his head was turned by his father's theatrical friends and 'the praise of the pious continued to feed his vanity . . . Montgomery had no talent whatsoever, only a fatal fluency in florid versification'. Nevertheless, he made enough from his books to attend Lincoln College, Oxford, graduating in 1833 and being ordained in 1835.

Queries out of context

Enquiries of this kind often come with a very meagre context, which even the most painstaking reference interview may still fail to elicit. Enquirers may not remember where they encountered the problem, or sometimes, for reasons of their own, may not wish to say.

Case 38: When asked what 'Bradbury's' were the librarian politely asked the enquirer where he had come across the word. He replied that he had read it somewhere and he couldn't find it in the dictionary. The librarian was pleased to find it immediately in the first place he looked, *New Britannica*, under the entry for 'Bradbury of Winsford, John Swanswick, 1st Baron', a civil servant and financial adviser to successive prime ministers and chancellors of the exchequer during World War I. 'As joint permanent secretary to the treasury (from 1913) he signed the first British £1 and 10s. notes (replacing gold coins at the beginning of World War I) which were known as "Bradbury's" for some years afterward.'

[It is true that the word 'Bradbury' is not in the *Concise Oxford dictionary* (7th edition, 1982), or in *Collins' dictionary* (1979) or in the *Longman dictionary* (1978), three recent and widely used British desk dictionaries. But of course these works are confined, respectively, to 'current English', 'English in general use', and 'contemporary English'. Neither is the word found in the great *Oxford English dictionary*, because the relevant alphabetical section was published in 1888. But it can be found, with explanation, in the 1972 *Supplement* to the *OED*, covering A to G, where the earliest use quoted is from *Punch*, 24th October 1914.]

Case 39: When asked, 'Can you find me a description of a planchette?', the librarian thought he detected, most unusually, some degree of reluctance in the enquirer to furnish further information. Still with no idea what a planchette was, therefore, he sensibly consulted the encyclopedias. He had no success with *New Britannica, Americana, World book* or *Academic American/Macmillan family*, but in *Collier's* index he came across an entry for 'planchet'. This led him to the article 'numismatics', defined as 'the study of coins', where he learned that it was a special term for 'the piece of metal prepared for striking'.

But this by no means suited his enquirer, who was quite positive that this was not what he wanted, while somewhat shamefacedly maintaining that he could not tell the librarian any more about what he did want. A possible reason for this reluctance did offer itself, however, when the librarian found the desired description in *Chambers's*: 'A thin piece of wood mounted on three props, two of which are furnished with castors, while one is a pencil which may be made to trace characters by resting the fingers on the instrument. Its use is as a medium for automatic writing and supposed spiritualist communications.' Double checking with *Everyman's*, he found a similar account, with the added note that, 'It is named after a French spiritualist who invented it in 1853.'

[*Collier's* does in fact have a five-line paragraph devoted to a good, clear description of a planchette and its uses in the article 'Fortune telling and divination', but though its 400,000-entry index is generally regarded as the best of any encyclopedia, it fails to include an entry for 'planchette'. And *Everyman's*, despite its reputation for scholarship, differs in its attribution of origin from the *Oxford English dictionary* which simply derives it from the

French word *planchette*, 'small board', a diminutive of *planche*, 'plank'. A check with the seven-volume *Grand Larousse de la langue française* (1976) shows that *planchette* has been used in French since the end of the 13th century.]

Stage two: analysing the subject
Having determined precisely what the reader requires, the librarian will then often find it necessary to make a detailed analysis of the subject of the question. It is essential to place the topic in its correct spot on the map of knowledge. A powerful weapon in reaching the heart of a problem, and one which falls particularly comfortably to the hand of the librarian, is classification. The analysis of a subject, which classification demands, not only allows the librarian to see it more clearly in its context but often suggests keywords to search in bibliographies and indexes. Facet analysis in particular enables the librarian speedily to break down any problem, however complex.

Case 40: So far as concerned the precise subject of an enquiry received in an academic library, the librarian felt no need to probe further: his reader wanted to know something about the Vivaldi sonata discovered in a north of England library about ten years earlier. But he did pause for a moment to survey the cluster of concepts making up the question as stated – each suggesting an approach to solving the problem: via music sources, obviously, both encyclopedic and bibliographical; or by way of biographical sources on Vivaldi himself; or by date, *circa* 1975; or through the library literature; or by place, as yet only vaguely defined.

As a first step, he checked the 15-page article on Vivaldi by Michael Talbot in the *New Grove dictionary of music and musicians*, published in 1980, which was of course sufficiently recent to have taken account of any finds. He could trace no reference to the discovery, but was provided with a number of suggestions for further search: a good half of the article comprised a detailed list of Vivaldi's works and a bibliography, both compiled by Peter Ryom, whose own *Verzeichnis der Werke Antonio Vivaldis* (1974, with supplement 1979) had been described by

Talbot as 'the most complete, accurate and rationally organized catalogue that has so far appeared'. Conversely, the librarian noted that the two most recent books on Vivaldi listed by Ryom were both by Talbot.

As the library had copies of neither Ryom's *Verzeichnis* nor his *Les manuscrits de Vivaldi*, noted as 'in preparation', the librarian decided to try the approach by date, starting with periodical articles. The obvious source to consult was the monthly *Music index*, described as 'a subject–author guide to current music periodical literature'. A few moments with the annual cumulations around the year 1975 located the entry in the 1974 volume, 'Manuscripts of 12 Vivaldi sonatas (Henry Watson Music Library, Manchester)', with a reference to the *Musical times* for October 1974. Disappointingly, this turned out to be no more than a three-and-a-half line note, tucked away at the bottom of a page; interestingly, however, it reported that the discoverer was Michael Talbot himself.

Obviously the next step was to consult his books, both called *Vivaldi*, one dated 1978, the other 1979. The later work, the first of a new series of 'BBC Music Guides', was a paperback of 112 pages, but had no mention of Manchester in the index. The 1978 volume, one of the 'Master Musicians Series' had four mentions, which the librarian followed up one by one. He read that the discovery comprised a partly autograph set of twelve violin sonatas (seven hitherto entirely unknown and the rest known only in incomplete or variant form) as well as two violin concertos. The book had probably belonged to Cardinal Ottoboni in Rome or Venice. A brief half-page account was given of the music itself, and there was a reproduction (not indexed) of an actual page from the volume showing corrections in Vivaldi's own hand.

[Talbot's article in the *New Grove* does in fact mention the sonatas, but without saying they are recent discoveries: 'a handsome volume of violin sonatas in Manchester can be traced back to Ottoboni's library'.]

Stage three: the search strategy

Time spent on deep analysis of multifaceted problems is usually well repaid at the third stage of the reference process, the determination of a search strategy. Basically, this means deciding on the order in which each of the various sources available will be consulted. Of course, a step-by-step check through all of them (even in random order) will eventually produce the answer, if it is available, but the experienced librarian uses short cuts. The actual point of entry and the subsequent path are determined by the analysis of the question and previous knowledge of the sources. This is the heart of the reference process.

Experienced workers will tell you that this is the area where a librarian's flair is seen. Defined by the *Concise Oxford dictionary* as 'selective instinct', it will often lead along the most likely path to the goal almost without the searcher realizing it. Few would doubt that there is this instinctive element in much reference work, but as F. S. Stych has pointed out, even those intuitive leaps and irrational hunches which can often lead to a problem's solution are 'probably the result of a rapid, subconscious review of stored knowledge'.

Stage four: the search
The search proper, which makes up the fourth stage, comprises the actual examination of the available sources of information as determined by the search strategy. Obviously these sources will vary considerably from library to library: in some industrial libraries, correspondence files are a major source to be included in the routine of any exhaustive search, but in many university libraries such files play practically no part at all. With unpublished university theses, the converse is true. For librarians lacking experience of reference work, and not yet sure that they possess this flair, deciding on the point at which they break into this circle of information sources is perhaps the most difficult professional decision they will have to face. And little can be offered to them by way of advice. There is no standard search method that can be followed. If their knowledge of the sources does not suggest a place to look, and if the obvious starting point, the catalogue, is either inappropriate or has failed them, there are two courses open to them. Firstly, they can follow the old reference librarian's maxim: 'The encyclopedia is the place to look if you can't think of a place to look.' They will be pleasantly surprised how often the great general encyclopedias will prove helpful, even if they

do no more than give a lead. This is particularly so with fact-finding enquiries.

Case 41: 'What's the latest date for Easter?' was a question that could have been answered by a more knowledgeable librarian from a variety of sources (*Whitaker's almanack, Brewer's dictionary of phrase and fable*, the *Oxford dictionary of the Christian church*) but the assistant in a college library decided to try the encyclopedias first. Immediately in the *Micropaedia* volumes of *New Britannica* she found a clear explanation of how Easter is calculated (in the West): 'The first Sunday after the full moon that occurs upon or next after the vernal equinox (March 21).' The effect of this is that Easter can fall at any time between 22nd March and 25th April.

She also pointed out to the enquirer the later sentence: 'In the Eastern Orthodox Church, however, a slightly different calculation is followed, with the result that the Orthodox Easter . . . can fall one, four, or five weeks later.'

Secondly, and much more than past generations, inexperienced librarians unsure where to start can call to their aid the systematic bibliography of that area that is particularly their own – reference materials (including bibliographies). In E. P. Sheehy, *Guide to reference books* and *Walford's guide to reference material* (now with its vastly improved subject indexing) they have two immensely powerful search tools, encompassing over 30,000 titles between them.

Case 42: The young librarian in the reference library of a London borough could not immediately think of any source that would give her the price of coal per ton in 1892. After a moment's irresolution she reached for *Walford's guide*, selecting the social and historical sciences volume. The index guided her to the section on statistics, where she focused her attention on the dozen or so titles under 'Great Britain'. The most promising source seemed to be B. R. Mitchell and P. Deane, *Abstract of British historical* *statistics* (1962): the annotation indicated that section 4 was devoted to coal and section 16 to prices, and that there was an analytical index. It was to this index she turned first when she consulted the library's copy: under 'coal: prices' she was directed to nine pages of tables, one of which was headed 'Annual average price of best coal in London . . . 1831–1938 (per ton)'. The figure for 1892 was 18 shillings and 6 pence. Judging from her enquirer's age that he would be familiar with pre-decimalization currency she felt she had no need to convert it for him (to 92½ pence).

Four basic sources, however, are common to all libraries: the library catalogue; bibliographical sources (including lists, indexes and abstracts of periodicals); reference materials (such as encyclopedias, dictionaries, yearbooks and directories); and the literature in the field. The young librarian should note, however, that many enquiries for their solution require the hunt to be pursued in and out of the various categories of sources, as the twisting course taken by the problem requires.

Case 43: In the hope of a quick answer the librarian in a county library headquarters tried the encyclopedias first when asked for the meaning of the stripes on a sailor's collar. In *New Britannica* he could find nothing on naval uniforms at all; in *Collier's* and *Americana* he found illustrations of US Navy and Royal Navy ratings wearing the distinctive collar with its three white stripes, but no explanation; in *Everyman's* he read that, 'The sailor collar dates its origin from the time when sailors wore "pigtails" and prevented the latter from soiling the uniform.' The first gleam of light came from *Chambers's* which gave the date of its introduction as 1857: 'The British naval uniform of . . . square blue collar with white bands . . . has spread with minor variations to virtually every navy in the world.' Cited in the references was D. Jarrett, *British naval dress* (1960).

When the library copy was traced it was found to be a 159-page work with over a hundred black-and-white illustrations. The librarian noted the author's claim that 'Relatively little has been written about naval dress', echoed by the publisher's blurb that 'this absorbing branch of naval history has never previously been dealt with comprehensively'. Disappointed to find no index entry under 'collar', the librarian was thumbing through the pages when, as so often happens, the words 'blue jean collar' sprang out at him. Following up the half-dozen page references given he learned that in the 1840s there was no officially authorized uniform, but the royal yacht uniform set the standard for others to follow with a 'broad blue collar edged with three white lines. . . . This is the uniform which popularized the "sailor suit" for children'. Pressing on, he read further: 'In 1845 an issue of blue jean and Dutch tape was authorized . . . but no indication was given as to the number of rows of tape to be put round the collar.' An 1856 committee under the chairmanship of a rear-admiral recommended two rows, but when the Admiralty consulted the commanders-in-chief at Portsmouth and Devonport they found a majority of captains in favour of 'three rows of white tape, three sixteenths of an inch in width and set one eighth of an inch apart'. In their Circular no. 283 of 30th January 1857 the Lords Commissioners stated their desire that 'these regulation articles of dress be worn'.

The enquirer was obviously fascinated by all this curious detail but did make the comment: 'But it doesn't say what the stripes mean', which the librarian had to admit was so. Leaving him with Jarrett, the librarian went to consult *Walford's guide to reference material* in search of the appropriate reference book on naval uniforms. To his surprise, he could find no specific work on the topic, though naval uniforms were included with army and air force uniforms in R. Knotel, *Uniforms of the world* (1980), which the library did not possess. There had been nothing on naval uniforms other than Jarrett on the open shelves so his next step was to consult the subject catalogue. All he found were two pamphlets, G. Dickens, *The dress of the British sailor* (2nd edition, 1977) with 24 pages and R. J. Wilkinson-Latham, *The Royal Navy, 1790–1970* (1977) with 40 pages. These he retrieved from the stacks, noting that neither had an index. This of course was not surprising: neither of them was a reference book, 'designed by the arrangement and treatment of its subject matter to be consulted for definite items of information rather than to be read consecutively', as the *ALA glossary of library and information science* (1983) defines it. They were bright, attractive, illustrated booklets for the amateur enthusiast. The first, indeed, by a retired admiral and grandson of Charles Dickens, had been compiled for the National Maritime Museum and published by Her Majesty's Stationery Office. The librarian and his enquirer scanned it together. Within moments they found: 'A word about the collar. A legend arose, and still persists, that the three rows of white tape were to commemorate the three great victories of Nelson – the Nile, Copenhagen and Trafalgar. No such sentimental idea stirred the breasts of the people concerned at the Admiralty for, at one time, the merits of two stripes as against three were canvassed.' The pamphlet by Wilkinson-Latham, devoted entirely to uniforms despite its more general title, confirmed this: 'These lines had nothing to do with Nelson's victories, as legend supposes: the original recommendation was for two or four rows, and compromise made it three.' By way of a bonus it also reproduced a Winterhalter painting (c.1846) showing the young Prince Albert Edward (later King Edward VII) in a sailor suit with three stripes on the collar, the summer rig of the royal yacht.

The librarian and his enquirer eventually concluded that the stripes on the collar had no special meaning; as Dickens explained, long before the 1857 regulations 'the sailors invariably made decorative additions to their new collars . . . piping . . . braid trimming . . . and so forth'.

[Each of the three works consulted would have been revealed by a search of the *British national bibliography* subject index under 'uniforms: ratings: Great Britain: Royal Navy . . .' (Dickens); 'Uniforms: Great Britain: Royal Navy . . .' (Wilkinson-Latham); 'uniforms: naval forces' (Jarrett). The work by Jarrett (incorrectly spelt Jarret in both text and index) is in the third edition of Walford (1975), though evidently dropped from the fourth.]

Colleagues as a resource

In a category of its own is a fifth source: the library staff. The collective experience and accumulated knowledge of a good staff are major assets in any library, and should be drawn on as a matter of course. Some libraries have an unwritten rule that no reader should be turned away without an answer until all the staff have had a chance to contribute to the search. Queries about quotations, local matters, current affairs, and of course about any special subject, are instances where colleagues can often help even after all documentary sources have failed. And if, as in some libraries, an attempt is made to formalize some of this accumulated experience in a staff information index, query file, etc., this becomes a further source to be considered in any routine search.

Case 44: When asked what it was that in Italy is 'cam', in Germany is 'z', and in France is 'ch', the young assistant's first thought was that these were abbreviations. But when she had failed to find them in K. Guinagh, *Dictionary of foreign phrases and abbreviations* (3rd edition, 1983), or in E. T. Crowley, *International acronyms, initialisms and abbreviations dictionary* (1984), which also concerns itself specifically with foreign abbreviations, etc., he began to wonder if he had jumped to the wrong conclusion. Wisely, he consulted a senior colleague. Her first reaction was to suspect a competition query; her second, after a moment's reflection was, 'Yes, of course, they are all abbreviations for "room". You find them used in hotel guides: "camera", "Zimmer", "chambre".'

Outside sources and referral

A reference librarian's familiarity with the sources of information should not be confined to those within the walls of one library. No library can ever be self-sufficient and outside sources need to be regularly drawn upon to satisfy the needs of enquirers. Commonly, librarians will consult other sources directly, usually by phone, on behalf of their own enquirers. Online searching is merely the latest manifestation of this practice. Increasingly too a librarian will pass on or refer an enquirer to an outside source more able to solve a particular problem.

Case 45: Asked in a university library what commodities make up the Cost of Living Index the librarian could find nothing in the library catalogue on the subject. Turning to that most universal of single-volume reference books, *Whitaker's almanack*, he was immediately guided to over half-a-page on the topic, including a probable explanation for the absence of any mention in the catalogue. It was first calculated in 1914, but 'since 1947 the Index of Retail Prices has superseded the cost-of-living index, although the older term is still popularly applied to it'. The actual index was shown for the years 1914 to 1982, and it was explained that 'a representative list of items is selected and the prices actually charged for these items are collected at regular intervals'. But no indication was given as to what these items were.

Clearer now as to exactly what he was looking for the librarian turned to the *Annual abstract of statistics* where the index entry 'retail prices index' led him to a table covering the last 17 years with separate figures for ten groups of commodities, e.g., food, fuel and light, services. This was plainly a step in the right direction but was not sufficiently detailed for the enquirer. In search of more detail the librarian next consulted the highly-praised Central Statistical Office *Guide to official statistics* (4th edition, 1982), awarded the Library Association Besterman Medal for an outstanding bibliography or guide. This explained that 'The prices of some 600 goods and services are regularly collected and approximately 130,000 separate price quotations are used each month in compiling the index.' Cited was *Methods of construction and calculation of the Index of Retail Prices*, published in 1967 by HMSO, but a note warned, 'This booklet is now out of print. An up-dated version is in process of preparation.' A copy was traced in the library and appendix A was found to comprise a list of some 350 separate commodities, e.g., self-raising flour, tennis racket, whisky per nip and per bottle, writing paper. It was obvious from some of the items included that this list had been overtaken by events, but the librarian felt he had gone as far as he could with the resources at his disposal. What he did strongly recommend to his enquirer, however, was the list of 'Government department contact points' at the end of the *Guide to official statistics*, with its invitation to ask them for 'further information and advice'. Together they identified the appropriate point to contact as the Department of Employment, with its address and phone number, including the specific extension to call about the Index of Retail Prices.

Intuition

Mention has already been made of the role intuition can play in reference work. This of course cannot be explained, and it occurs unplanned, but no experienced reference librarian can deny that it happens. Perhaps H. L. Mencken has come closest to describing what it is: 'Some impenetrable and intangible talent for guessing correctly.'

Case 46: When asked in a public reference library for a copy of 'The Derby ram' the librarian knew intuitively that it was a poem. Thinking about it afterwards she could not explain why – logically of course it could have been about sheep-rearing, or a novel, or even a book about Derby County Football Club ('The Rams'). Clearly her subconscious may have played a part.

She went unhesitatingly to *Granger's index to poetry* where she was given nine locations. She chose the *Faber book of nonsense verse*. The poem was found to have six stanzas, beginning, 'As I was going to Derby, / 'Twas on a market day, / I saw the finest ram, sir, / That ever was fed on hay.'

[The fact that another location given is the *Oxford nursery rhyme book* suggests that the librarian may have instinctively recalled a forgotten childhood memory.]

Another asset that experience brings to the reference librarian is what G. R. James calls 'a developed sense of probability'. This is helpful with those many enquiries where 'proof beyond a reasonable doubt' is lacking. It is comforting for the librarian to know that the law also recognizes a second, lower, standard of 'proof on the balance of probabilities'.

Case 47: The librarian asked for the address of the 'Welsh Harp' in London guessed that it was a 'pub', which the enquirer confirmed: 'It's quite a famous one', he added. The 'Alphabetical directory (commercial and professional)' section of the current *Kelly's Post Office London directory* listed two Welsh Harps, each designated 'public house' (as well as a Welsh Harp Boat Centre and a Welsh Harp Service Station). The address of the first public house was 32 Homerton Row E9, and of the second, 47 Chandos Place WC2. The postal district numbers indicated that the two houses were in very different parts of London, but the enquirer was unable to indicate which was the one he wanted – though he did reveal that he had arranged to meet an old friend there.

Turning to the 'Street directory' section in search of a map reference the librarian was able to locate in turn each Welsh Harp on the map incorporated in the volume. The E9 house was in the East End, a few streets from Hackney Marshes, the WC2 house was in the West End, close to Trafalgar Square. While the enquirer still hesitated over which one he should choose for his rendezvous, the librarian decided that the balance of probability lay with the West End Welsh Harp. His enquirer agreed.

[An alternative place to look would have been the London phone book, but this does not list the WC2 Welsh Harp, and gives no indication that the E9 Welsh Harp is indeed a public house.]

Alternative approaches

It should be emphasized that all search strategies must be flexible, and subject to modification at any time in the light of what the search itself reveals (or fails to reveal). Indeed, pauses for evaluation should be planned as a feature of all search strategies.

In attempting to come to grips with an enquiry the experienced reference librarian frequently finds that certain secondary approaches suggest themselves. J. I. Wyer describes these as 'handles that may be laid hold of' in studying or working towards the solution of a problem. The primary direction for the search of course will be indicated by the subject, but the approach from one of these secondary angles may well produce the result more speedily. Again the choice of a particular line to pursue in an individual case is largely a matter of reference instinct, but the most useful 'handles' to consider are person, date, place and form.

Approach by person

A number of questions are susceptible to attack from this angle, for example, enquiries on inventions and quotations. It is a good rule to try the biographical angle first if possible because biography is a field comparatively well-documented.

Case 48: The enquirer in an east coast reference library, a Sunday school teacher, was working on the history of the Sunday school movement, but had been unable to find anything useful in the library catalogue. The reference librarian struck lucky immediately with a full-page article in *Chambers's encyclopaedia*, mainly historical. The enquirer studied this with interest, but then returned for more. Checking the bibliography at the foot of the article the librarian read, 'A comprehensive history of the Sunday school movement remains to be written; there are histories of individual schools.' Of the two items cited one was just such an individual history, and the other was a book on the modern Sunday school. Glancing back over the article the librarian noted that 'the beginnings of the Sunday school movement in its modern sense are usually associated with the work begun in 1780 by Robert Raikes, printer and proprietor of the *Gloucester Journal*'. The index had referred her to another article; this turned out to be a separate entry devoted to Raikes. She found three works cited at the end: A. Gregory, *Robert Raikes* (1877); J. H. Harris, *Robert Raikes: the man and his work* (1899); G. Kendall, *Robert Raikes: a critical study* (1933). Librarian and reader both decided that this was a line worth pursuing. The first and third were in the catalogue, and a check under Raikes produced a fourth, too recent for *Chambers's*, F. Booth, *Robert Raikes of Gloucester* (1980).

The work by Gregory (the library's edition was dated 1880) was in fact subtitled *a history of the origin of Sunday schools*, and its 189 pages were almost entirely on that subject rather than on Raikes himself. They noted that there was no bibliography. Kendall's work was found to be 'First published 1939' and not 1933 as *Chambers's* had it. It contained a useful two-page bibliography and referred to Harris (published in Bristol) as 'the principal authority'. The book by Booth was a scholarly historical account, with extensive endnotes.

At this point the librarian felt she could leave her enquirer to get on with it, but as a last check she looked under 'Raikes' in the British Library *General catalogue of printed books*, where she found C. R. Newby, *The story of Sunday schools: Robert Raikes and after* (1930). When in due course a copy was obtained she found that it was not quite the history that she had hoped for, but a pious inspirational account of 48 pages without a bibliography. She did note with interest, however, that it had been 'written for that great body of Sunday school teachers who are the lineal descendants of Robert Raikes'.

Approach by date
The establishment of even an approximate date can provide the key to the solution of many enquiries. The reason for this is simple. Many of the sources used by the librarian are assembled on the shelves in date order: bibliographies, periodical indexes (and of course the periodicals themselves), yearbooks and directories, many sources of biographical reference, special indexes to patent specifications, parliamentary papers, etc.

Case 49: 'Can you tell me when the last burning at the stake was?' was the question asked in a public reference library. 'You mean in this country?' was the librarian's necessary response. Assured that it was the last occurrence in England that interested the enquirer the librarian turned confidently to the various dictionaries of dates: the venerable *Haydn's dictionary of dates* had a few lines on 'burning alive', the last victim mentioned being Elizabeth Gaunt burnt at Tyburn for treason on 23rd October 1684. The two-volume H. R. Keller, *Dictionary of dates* (1934) lacks an index and so was unsuited for an enquiry of this kind. Nothing at all on the topic could be traced in *Everyman's dictionary of dates* (6th edition, 1971) or in the *Teach yourself encyclopaedia of dates and events* (1968), but in *Hamlyn dictionary of dates and anniversaries* (2nd edition, 1978) she read, under 'burning to death', that this was the 'punishment in England for women convicted of certain crimes, last inflicted 1789; legally abolished 1790'.

As she half expected, however, this exact answer to the enquirer's question only served to increase his interest. He wished to know more – who it was, what was she executed for, and an account, if possible. The encyclopedias were obviously worth a try: the index to the most likely British set, *Chambers's*, was silent about burnings at the stake; *New Britannica* and *Americana*, the largest encyclopedias, had the briefest mentions. It crossed the librarian's mind that this was just the kind of detail that might be found in the old and in many respects still unsurpassed 11th edition of *Britannica* of 1910–11. She was rewarded by an article of over 50 lines on 'burning to death', beginning, 'As a legal punishment for various crimes burning alive was formerly very widespread.' Confirmation was provided of the date of the last occurrence, but no name or other details were given. She was appalled to read why it was particularly applied to women: it was considered more 'decent' than the alternative suffered by men, hanging and exposure on a gibbet.

A change of direction was called for, and possession of a date suggested where she should look: the appropriate volume in what *Walford's guide* calls the 'monumental' series issued by the American Historical Association and the Royal Historical Society of Great Britain, *Bibliography of British history, 1789–1851* (1977). Subject entries in the index were sparse, so she consulted the extensive 19 pages of contents, soon tracing the sub-section 'Capital punishment'. There she found seven titles listed, of which the most promising was J. Lawrence, *A history of capital punishment with special reference to capital punishment in Great Britain* (1932). When the library's copy was examined, surprisingly few of its 256 pages of text dealt with burning alive, though there were two illustrations of women at the stake. It did, however, identify the last victim as Christian Murphy, convicted of coining, who suffered at the Old Bailey in 1789. The three-page bibliography made grim reading, though it had nothing specific on burning alive or on Christian Murphy, but now possessed of a name the librarian had other sources to explore.

She was immediately successful with the British Library *General catalogue of printed books*, where the entry under 'Murphy, Christian' directed her to 'Bowman, Christian' and a contemporary account, published in London in 1789: *The life and death of Christian Bowman, alias Murphy; who was burnt at a stake, in the Old Bailey . . . the 18th of March, 1789, for high treason in . . . counterfeiting the silver coin of the realm* [with "The Last Farewell to the World of the unfortunate Mrs. Bowman". In verse].

[A check of the cumulated indexes to the remarkable *Notes and queries* would quickly have located a note in the issue for 19th June 1909 confirming 'the last case on record' as Christian Bowman, with a reference to W. Andrews, *Bygone punishments* (1899).]

Approach by place

With many questions, place is an important as date. Even a hint as to location is worth following up, because, like biography, topography is a well-documented field. To take one example, when searching for biographical details on minor English figures of earlier centuries, the topographical volumes of the Victoria County Histories are a mine of information, once a connection can be established such as birthplace or property in a particular village, town or even county.

Case 50: Surprisingly to some perhaps, when asked for the inscription on Robin Hood's tombstone, the reference librarian consulted the *Dictionary of national biography*. She remembered having read somewhere that he was included, and indeed she found an entry seven columns in length, beginning 'legendary outlaw, has been represented as a historical personage'. But then she went on to read in the body of the article that 'The arguments in favour of Robin Hood's historical existence, though very voluminous, will not bear scholarly examination.' Nevertheless, she eventually found what she was hoping for: 'Thoresby, in his "Ducatus Leodiensis" (1715), p. 91, described a tombstone near Kirklees with an illegible inscription as the hero's grave.'

Though the library did not possess a copy of this 18th-century work, the librarian felt sure she could solve the problem by following up the lead provided by the place name. She was immediately successful with the first work she consulted, L. H. Fisher, *A literary gazetteer of England* (1980). The entry for Kirklees, Yorkshire began, 'This tiny village on the Calder River in the West Riding of Yorkshire, 2 miles from Brighouse, contains the remains of a Cistercian nunnery founded in 1155 . . . the traditional scene of the death of Robin Hood.' The article went on to describe the site of the grave, in the middle of a stand of trees, enclosed by iron railings, with a broken block of stone, and the 'much debated inscription'. This was quoted in full, six lines in length, beginning, 'Hear Underneath dis laitle Stean/ Las Robert earl of Huntingdon', and ending with the date of death, 24th December 1247.

Approach by form
The possibility of an approach via a particular form of information is usually obvious from the question: a request about inventions, for example, should immediately suggest patents; an enquiry for an address clearly indicates a directory. The librarian must remain on the alert for any question where the form approach may be helpful.

Case 51: When asked, 'Is it true that we spend more in one year on gambling than the whole cost of Trident?' the librarian recognized that this was one of those very common cases where the enquirer is seeking to prove a controversial point. He knew from experience that, for obvious reasons, accurate statistics on gambling were hard to come by, but he did not anticipate quite the difficulties he would encounter. There was no index entry for 'gambling' in either *Whitaker's almanack* or the *Annual abstract of statistics*, and though the current issue of *Social trends* did have some statistics on the numbers of betting offices, bingo clubs, casino gaming clubs and gaming machines, and some account of the sums staked, there was no total figure given. The best he could come up with was an approximation in the current year's *Britain: an official handbook*: 'The total money staked in Great Britain in 1981 was about £5,924 million.'

He appeared more immediately successful with the other half of the equation when he found an entry in *Whitaker's almanack* index under 'Trident Missile System', but at the page cited, 361, he could find no mention. After trying various permutations of the digits without success he abandoned the volume and turned to the *Annual abstract of statistics* and to *Britain*. Though defence expenditure received extensive treatment in both, Trident was not mentioned – and the librarian remembered that it was not a current system but one planned for the 1990s. A moment's further thought, particularly about the great controversy the proposal had aroused, suggested an obvious source for what he was seeking – the debates in Parliament.

Working backwards through the excellent indexes to the volumes of *Parliamentary debates (Hansard): House of Commons official report*, he quickly located a question asked in the House on 30th June 1983 by an MP seeking the 'latest estimate of the cost of the Trident II D5 weapons system'. The Minister's answer referred the honourable member to an earlier answer of 14th December 1982, where the librarian found the figure given as '£7,500 million, less several hundred million pounds as a result of the decision to process the missiles in the United States'.

Pointing out that both sets of figures were estimates, and not absolutely current, the librarian left his enquirer to make what he would of them.

[How complex an apparently simple statistical query can become was illustrated when on 30th January 1985 the Secretary of State for Defence gave the House of Commons a later estimate of the cost of Trident: £9,285 million, based on an established convention that assumed a dollar exchange rate of $1.38 to the pound. The laughter this provoked from the Opposition was no doubt occasioned by the fact that the actual exchange rate on that day in both London and New York stood at $1.11.]

Stage five: the response
In most cases such searches do produce an answer to the enquirer's question. But this is not the end of the story. As was said right at the beginning of this section, reference work is more than simply finding answers to questions. It is far more a matter of problem-solving. Thus in the final stage of the reference process it is necessary for the librarian to be sure not only that the question has been answered, but also that the response has satisfied the enquirer, and then in addition that the original problem has been solved. Only when assurance is forthcoming on each of these three counts can the reference librarian know that the task is complete.

INDEX

Of all the individual works mentioned in the text only those that have major significance as general reference or bibliographical sources and indexed here. As for the cases themselves, although no attempt has been made at an exhaustive index of their subject matter, each is entered here under a single descriptive phrase (after the manner of Sherlock Holmes), e.g., Runic alphabet (case 4), Whale on the beach (case 33).